501
COOK'S
TIPS

PAMELA DONALD

501
COOK'S
TIPS

*Hints and tips to save you time
and money in the Kitchen*

BCA

LONDON   NEW YORK   SYDNEY   TORONTO

For Nadia Steele and Paloma

This edition published 1993
by BCA by arrangement with
Judy Piatkus (Publishers) Ltd

CN 6999

Printed and bound in Great Britain by
Biddles Ltd, Guildford and King's Lynn

Contents

Introduction	page	ix
1 Meat (1–31)		1
Buying and Storing		1
Cooking		3
Economy Measures		4
Offal		5
Bacon, Gammon and Ham		6
Leftovers		7
And Yorkshire Pudding . . .		8
2 Poultry and Game (32–42)		9
Chicken, Turkey and Duck		9
Game		11
3 Fish and Shellfish (43–55)		12
Fresh and Smoked Fish		12
Shellfish		13
4 Barbecues (56–69)		15
Equipment and Coals		15
Barbecue Foods		16
5 Vegetables (70–141)		18
In General		18
Legumes		20
Green Vegetables		21
Root and Other Vegetables		22
Tomatoes		25
Potatoes		26
Onions		30
Garlic		31
6 Salads and Salad Dressings (142–172)		33
Salad Leaves		33
Other Salad Ingredients		36
Salad Dressings		39
7 Flavourings (173–189)		41
Condiments		41
Herbs		42
Spices		44

8 Fruit and Nuts (190–233)   45
   Dried Fruit   45
   Apples and Other Fruit   46
   Soft Summer Fruits   49
   Citrus Fruits   50
   Nuts   53

9 Eggs (234–262)   55
   In General   55
   Boiling Eggs   57
   Poaching Eggs   59
   Scrambled Eggs and Omelettes   59

10 Dairy Foods (263–295)   61
   Milk   61
   Cream   62
   Butter   63
   Yoghurt   65
   Cheese   66

11 Sauce Making (296–306)   68
   White Sauces and Variations   68
   Egg-Based Sauces   69

12 Pasta, Rice and Cereals (307–327)   72
   Pasta   72
   Rice   73
   Cereals   75

13 Bread and Baking (328–365)   77
   Bread and Scones   77
   Pastry   80
   Biscuits   82
   Meringues   83

14 Cakes (366–388)   86
   In General   86
   Fruit Cakes   87
   Sponge and Other Cakes   88
   Cake Icing and Decorating   89

15 Puddings and Sweet Things (389–409)   91
   Hot and Cold Puds   91
   Sweet Things   93

16 Jams and Preserves (410–424)   96
   Jams   96
   Marmalades   98
   Other Preserves   99

17 Entertaining (425–444)   100
   Special Occasions   100
   Christmas   102

18 Drinks (445–461)   105
   Alcoholic and Non-Alcoholic   105
   Coffee, Tea and Chocolate   107

19 Don't Panic (462–474)   109
   In an Emergency   109
   Emergency Substitutes   111

20 Essentials for Chief Cook and Bottle Washer   112
   (475–501)
   Gadgets and Equipment   112
   Cleaning and Washing Up   114

Introduction

I have always loved to cook, dating from my carefree bachelor-girl days in a pocket-sized London flat, and the discovery of spaghetti bolognaise. I became rather good at it, probably because it was the only thing I ever cooked, and we know that practice makes perfect. I only learned to do other things when I got married and after dreaming one night that he had drowned in a bowl of pasta, my husband treated me to a Cordon Bleu course and whisked me off to the Middle East. There I learned the wonders of curries from Goanese cooks and became quite obsessive again until I could prepare them in my sleep. There is a point to all this.

One Sunday on our first leave from the Gulf, old friends John and Jo Sandilands telephoned to say that they were practically on our doorstep in Suffolk. They were staying with a couple who lived only a few miles away and when John suggested that they all popped over for a pre-lunch drink, I insisted they should stay to eat with us.

'Wonderful,' he replied, 'you'll like the Wynn-Jones's. She's Delia Smith, the cookery writer, you know and . . .'

'Forget it.' I said. 'Drinks around noon then?'

But he insisted. Lunch it was. I then did a very foolish thing. Instead of sticking to the planned family fare of traditional roast lamb and summer pudding, I ran round like a headless chicken looking up borrowed recipes for spicy stuffed lamb and something out of the ordinary to follow. It was certainly that. In haste, I curdled the cream and undercooked the onions, but burned the garlic for the stuffing and overcooked the rice. Half a stone lighter by noon, I was forced to return to the original menu. It was a memorable summer's day and after a simple and easy-to-cook meal, we sat round the table way into the evening.

As I got to know Delia better, I confessed that I hadn't been looking forward to having her and described my earlier abortive efforts to impress.

'Can you imagine how much worse it is for me?' she asked. 'I can't afford any mistakes, everyone is expecting so much.'

And this was true when later she sent me a copy of her latest book with an invitation to dinner. I couldn't wait.

I remember duck cooked to crisp perfection. 'It's impossible to ruin,' she said, 'you don't have to keep an eye on the time, or keep popping out to the kitchen to baste it.' Other delights, all in line with the sensible policy of cooking today and eating tomorrow when entertaining, had been prepared in advance, but tasted mouth-wateringly fresh.

The object lesson has been that there is little point in having recipe books unless you know by heart the trade secrets of these 'supercooks', the age-old rescue remedies and modern-day devices to save time and money. Then cooking for a family, friends or business associates becomes pleasurable and affordable. Recently I admired a vast collection of obviously unused cookery books at the home of a busy working mother who said, 'What I keep looking for is one which tells me how I can cook for all occasions and wallpaper the walls at the same time.' Here it is.

Pamela Donald

Meat

Buying and Storing

1   If you live in an area with only a few expensive shops, you will save money by travelling to a more built-up area where cheaper butchers are vying for trade and catering for families on lower incomes. This is especially true when buying in bulk. If you have a freezer you can make super-savings anywhere by buying a whole or half carcass, and having it cut into joints and small portions.

2   Many shoppers buy the more expensive cuts of meat because these are the ones they know by name and find easiest to prepare. Cheaper cuts, however, often have more flavour, even if they might take longer to cook. Belly or neck end of pork, brisket, leg, flank, chuck and blade of beef, and breast or neck of lamb can be made into delicious and nourishing casseroles.

3   Meat and poultry which has been kept for some time or retained in its cling-film packaging after buying, can become strong smelling. A wipe with a clean cloth wrung out in a mixture of cold water and vinegar should remove the smell. If it doesn't, it's wisest to throw it away.

4   If you're worried about storing meat for a few days in the fridge, rub the outside with vinegar and/or dried mustard powder. This will not alter the flavour of the meat when cooked.

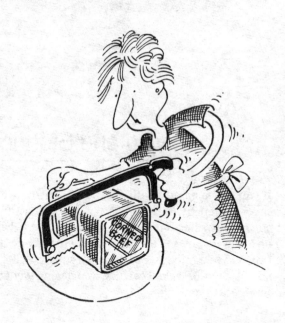

5   Keeping tinned meat in the fridge will make the contents easier to slice. If the tin is opened at both ends when needed, it's a simple matter to push the meat out undamaged.

Cooking

6 After coating meat, chicken or liver to be fried in seasoned flour, use any flour left over to thicken the pan juices for a sauce or gravy.

7 Adding flour and sliced onion to a roasting pan before the meat is put in is one way of ensuring a rich flavoured sauce which has absorbed all the cooking juices.

8 The quickest way to flour-coat cubes of meat for stews and casseroles is to place the flour, salt, pepper, and chopped herbs for flavour in a polythene bag. Pop the meat in and shake the bag vigorously to coat evenly. Then fry in hot fat to brown and 'seal' before adding the liquid.

9 Damp or wet meat won't brown when fried, and will spit and splash all over the pan. Always pat meat dry with kitchen paper before adding to hot fat. Meat pieces also become a watery grey colour instead of brown if too many are added to hot fat at once. This reduces the temperature of the fat, and the meat 'steams' rather than frying brown. Do only a few pieces at a time.

10 If you put a joint of meat on a rack in a roasting tin, the base will not shrink or overcook, and will provide an extra portion when served. Another benefit is that it is easier to remove excess fat from the meat.

11 Once a joint is cooked, leave it to rest for 10-15 minutes in a warm place before carving. The fibres of the meat will settle, and the carver's job will be that much easier. (This tip applies to poultry too.)

| 12 | To tenderise even the toughest steak, give it a good bashing with a rolling pin, meat pounder or hammer. Cover it with a piece of greaseproof paper or baking parchment first. |

| 13 | Raw meat will cut more easily if it is popped into the freezer for at least an hour or two before chopping or slicing. The best place to defrost wholly frozen meat is on a grill pan grid. This allows air to circulate all round it. |

| 14 | Add a tablespoon of vinegar to a curry or stew to help tenderise the cheapest cuts and bring out the flavours. Only add seasoning at the end of cooking a stew or roast. Salt draws juices from meat and can make it tough and rubbery. |

Economy Measures

| 15 | Healthy bulgar or cracked wheat or porridge oats used instead of flour will thicken runny stews and mince dishes and make them go further. About 2 tablespoons per 1lb (450g) of meat will do. |

| 16 | When making a meat loaf, try adding an individual serving packet of Rice Krispies to lighten the texture and add a little bulk. Or combine the mince with cheaper sausagemeat and/or minced mushrooms to stretch it. (*See also 472.*) |

| 17 | Cheaper cuts of meat like neck or shin normally need long, slow cooking. By investing in a mincer, you can mince them and cook quickly into dishes which are tastier, thriftier and less fatty than ready-prepared butchers' mince. To get the very last shred of meat from a mincer finish off by passing a slice of bread through the gadget. This also helps to clean it. |

18 Instant potato mix and packets of soup can be added to stretch runny meat, poultry or fish dishes as well as thickening them and adding extra flavour. For example oxtail and beef broth in meat stews; chicken and sweetcorn in chicken casseroles, and mushroom is particularly good with fish and pork.

Offal

19 Calves' and lambs' liver is much more expensive than pigs' or ox, but very much more tender and subtle in flavour. If you buy the cheaper varieties ask the butcher to slice them very thinly. Before cooking, soak these stronger-tasting, tougher slices in a little milk for about an hour. Drain well before drying on kitchen paper, then dusting with flour. The taste and texture will be much improved.

20 Excessive heat and prolonged cooking will ruin liver. When frying, cook quickly in an uncrowded pan. When done, the inside should still be slightly pink.

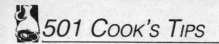

Bacon, Gammon and Ham

21 Cooking bacon in the oven without fat (or grilling it) is healthier than frying it. Rinse the slices under cold water for a few seconds, dry well with kitchen paper and arrange in an earthenware or enamel dish. Cook in a medium oven until done to taste.

22 If bacon has dried up or is too salty, soak it in milk for 10 minutes before blotting dry with paper towels and cooking.

23 Both bacon joints and bacon rashers taste delightfully different when brushed with a little runny honey before cooking.

24 When using bacon rashers as a wrapping for sausages, kidneys, prunes etc., first stretch each rasher on a chopping board using the back of a knife. Pull it as far as it will go. It won't shrink so much in cooking now, and of course the rashers will go a lot further.

25 To avoid the rashers in a plastic pack sticking together, roll the pack up and secure with a rubber band before storing in the fridge. If packs of rashers have been stored in the freezer, rolling and unrolling the pack a few times before opening will speed up the defrosting process. Slide a heated knife in to separate the slices as well. Blot well with kitchen paper to stop the bacon spitting in the pan.

26 │ You can quickly reduce the salt content of ham, bacon or gammon joints by placing them in cold water, bringing to the boil and immediately throwing the water and much of the salt out. Replace with fresh cold water, bring again to the boil, reduce to a simmer and continue to cook until tender. Where time permits, leave very salty joints in water overnight, changing the water several times before cooking. Leave boiled joints to cool in the cooking water before lifting on to a serving dish. They will carve more easily and be extra moist.

Leftovers

27 │ Leftover meat can be finely chopped or minced, then seasoned with a few herbs, or a dash of Tabasco or Worcestershire sauce. Depending on the amount it can then be used to stuff marrow, peppers, mushrooms, courgettes or savoury pancakes. Leftover meat can also be transformed into a quick chilli con carne by adding chilli paste or powder and a tin of red kidney beans. Always cook chilli powder in some oil first or it will taste raw.

28 │ Cut leftover roast meat into cubes and add to a curry sauce, to be served with rice; or mince it and mix with fried onion and tomatoes for a pasta sauce. Mixed with chopped cooked onion, herbs and a can of tomatoes or some gravy, sliced leftover meat can be topped with mashed potato to become Shepherd's or Cottage Pie (depending on whether you use lamb or beef). Such pies go down particularly well with children if a small can of baked beans is mixed in with the meat and gravy.

My all-time favourite leftover meat dish is stovies. We ate it regularly when I was a child in Scotland. Recipes vary but here's my old Scots mother's method and it's so good.

Cut up the leftover bits of roast, however scraggy and small.

Chop some onions and fry them in clarified meat dripping *(see 30)* until light golden brown. Add some sliced cooked potatoes and stir gently in before adding the meat. Cook for a few minutes, then add any leftover gravy. Bubble gently for a minute more and serve piping hot. This may not win awards from Weight Watchers or the British Heart Foundation, but it's unbeatable on a cold winter's day.

29   Meat and poultry bones which can't be used straightaway to make stock, can be kept in a polythene bag in the freezer until needed. They are far too valuable to throw away. After making a stock, boil to reduce it and concentrate its flavour. Pour the cooled liquid into a plastic freezer bag inside a freezer container (or margarine or ice-cream tub, depending on quantity) and freeze. Afterwards take the bag out of the container and have ready-made stock in easily stacked portions which can be returned to the freezer until needed. And the container is freed for another time. Smaller amounts of stock or leftover gravy can be frozen in ice-cube trays and then stored as cubes in plastic bags in the freezer.

30   To clarify dripping from roast meat, put the fat in a basin with just enough boiling water to cover it, and stir well as it softens and melts. When cool, the clarified dripping will solidify on top and this can be removed leaving a tasty liquid underneath. This is ideal for soups or gravy.

And Yorkshire Pudding

31   Lighten Yorkshire puddings by letting the batter stand and rest for an hour before adding to really hot fat in the tin. For a different flavour, you could add some dried or chopped fresh mixed herbs.

Poultry and Game

Chicken, Turkey and Duck

32 When shopping for the freezer, look for fresh chickens reduced in price because they're near their sell-by date. Freeze immediately. Ready-frozen birds can contain as much as 10% water.

33 Of course it's more convenient to buy chicken portions, but you pay dearly. It's much cheaper to buy whole birds and dissect them yourself. A little effort with a stout pair of kitchen shears or a sharp-bladed knife will produce breasts, thighs, drumsticks, wings and a carcass, giblets and other tasty bits for stock. Keep the livers from every chicken you buy in a plastic tub in the freezer. You will soon have enough for a pâté. The lumps of fat around the cavity opening of a chicken can be rendered down for chicken fat. Fry gently in a dry pan, and keep pressing to release the fat. Pour this off and use instead of oil or butter in cooking where appropriate. Store in the fridge.

34 For extra soft and succulent chicken breasts, soak the pieces in milk for a couple of hours.

35 He may look more comfortable perched in your roasting tin sunny side up, but if a chicken or turkey is cooked upside down, the juices will run into the breast which otherwise can dry out before the rest of the bird is cooked. The meat is not only kept moist, it will go further when carved.

36 Poultry is properly cooked if, when pricked with a skewer, colourless, not pink, juice runs out.

37 For a crispy duck skin, first dry the skin really well. Try a hair dryer, then rub the surface with salt. Ducks are notoriously fatty, so never add any extra fat, prick the skin at intervals in the cooking to let the fat run out. Pour this off at intervals, allow it to solidify, and use it up later in pâtés, for roasting potatoes etc. If you stuff a duck with a whole apple, this will absorb excess grease.

38 Cheaper but tougher boiling fowl should be soaked in un-salted cold water overnight. The next day cover with fresh water, add a tablespoon of vinegar, then bring to the boil and simmer until tender.

Game

39 If you like your game birds hung until the 'high' stage, test by pulling on a feather from the plumage at the lower back near the tail. It is ready to be cooked and eaten when the tail feathers come out easily.

40 If feathered game or poultry is first plunged into boiling water for about a minute, it will be easier to pluck. This also stops the feathers flying around.

41 To keep flies at bay while hanging game – for 1-3 weeks depending on the weather – sprinkle the birds with a home-made powder repellent. Simply mix equal parts of ground cloves, black pepper and flour together. Hang small birds by the neck, larger ones by the feet.

42 Always bard the breasts of game birds while cooking, as the flesh is very dry. Use very thin strips of pork fat, salt pork or unsmoked bacon.

Fish and Shellfish

Fresh and Smoked Fish

43   Ideally, fresh fish should be cooked and eaten as soon as possible after purchase. If it must be kept in the refrigerator for a day or so, rub salt over the fish, then wrap in a clean cloth dampened with vinegar. Over-wrap in an outer covering of kitchen foil.

44   Speed up a fish-scaling operation by first dipping the fish for 5 seconds in boiling water.

45   To skin fish more easily, dip your wet hands in salt. This will help you get a better grip.

46 To freeze fresh fish, either pop it in a milk carton topped up with water or wrap it in kitchen foil. The latter is better than plastic wrapper for retaining moisture during the freezing process. Fish should be thawed as slowly as possible for best results, but in an emergency place it in its sealed wrapper in cold water, or brush the surface of the frozen pieces with a little vinegar.

47 For a quick and delicious way to prepare salmon, plunge it into boiling water seasoned with a little lemon juice, salt and pepper and boil gently for 3 minutes per lb (450g). Cover and set aside to cool in the liquid.

48 Just as you would save meat and poultry bones for stock, so the trimmings left over when you fillet your own fish are invaluable for fish soups and sauces. Pop them in a sealed container, freeze and label them for future use.

49 Pop kippers in hot water for a minute before cooking to remove excessive oiliness without reducing the moisture content. Strongly tasting smoked kippers or those which have become dry will be restored to plumpness by soaking them in hot water for an hour. Dry them off well before cooking.

50 If you find anchovy fillets or smoked salmon too salty, soak in milk for half an hour. Dry well on kitchen paper.

Shellfish

51 Mussels should be bought live, with the shells closed. Keep in salted water in a basin or bucket and add a teaspoon of oatmeal; this will cause the mussels to release grit. Discard any that remain open after an hour; they are dead. Scrub the shells and remove any beards, then place the mussels in a bowl of freshly salted water into which stir half a cup of flour. Leave them in the fridge overnight to 'feed' on the flour. They will then be plump, clean and well rinsed, ready for cooking. When they are cooked, throw away any mussels which remain closed.

52 Unless shrimps are fresh from the sea, place them in a bath of vinegar for 20 minutes to improve the flavour. If shrimps or prawns have dried up a little, soak in milk to plump them up again. For an extra special flavour try marinating shrimps or prawns in a little port before cooking them.

53 Gentleman lobsters are smaller and go redder in cooking than hen lobsters, and it is the latter that are considered more delicate in flavour. Ready-cooked lobsters must have stiff tails – tired old lobsters have bendy tails.

54 Oyster shells aren't meant to be easy to open, so be suspicious of any which give way without a bit of resistance. The ubiquitous tin opener does a good job here, but be very careful to avoid accidents. And never serve whisky with oysters, as this can lead to dire stomach upsets.

55 The Mediterranean influence in cooking means that fishmongers are selling more octopus and squid than ever before. In Greece the flesh is beaten, but to tenderise these rather rubbery molluscs at home, toss a few corks in the cooking water.

Barbecues

Equipment and Coals

56 You'll spoil the taste of food if petrol or paraffin are used to light a barbecue. They may be cheap but they are also highly dangerous. White block firelighters or a little methylated spirits applied with due care are cheaper than proprietary brands of barbecue fuels, and are much less volatile. Allow them to burn out completely before you put food near them.

57 To reflect heat back to the food and speed up the cooking process, line the barbecue container with aluminium foil placed sunny side up, then add a layer of gravel or sand. (This also makes it easier to clean afterwards.)

58 Don't add new coals to the centre when the fire is becoming low, as this will considerably reduce the temperature. Push hot coals to the middle, and add the new coals to the outside.

59 A portable barbecue kit is the answer for picnics. At the first hint of sunny weather the shops are full of them, but a biscuit tin with the metal grid from a grill pan will do the same job.

60 Dried herbs which are past their best for everyday cooking can be put out with the barbecue kit rather than the rubbish. Sprinkle some on the charcoal towards the end of cooking for a mouthwatering aroma. Or use fresh sprigs – woody herbs like rosemary are good.

61 Mayonnaise applied on wodges of paper towel does an excellent job of cleaning up a dirt-encrusted barbecue grill, especially where it is still fractionally warm.

62 Meat to be barbecued should be marinated in a flavourful marinade for up to 12 hours before cooking *(see 69)*. The chosen flavours can permeate the meat, making it more succulent and sufficiently moist to do away with continual basting which produces flare-ups from the coals. At the very least meat must be well brushed with oil to prevent sticking. Oil the barbecue grid too.

63 To seal in the flavour and juices of barbecue meat, sear it on a grill placed about 3 inches (7.5cm) above the fire. The grill can then be raised a couple of inches for the remainder of the cooking.

Barbecue Foods

64 Speed up the cooking time of hamburgers by making a few holes in them with a skewer. The holes seal up during cooking, but they help to conduct the heat.

65 | Sausages are easier to turn and brown uniformly on all sides if first threaded on to a skewer.

66 | As a change from the traditional sausages and hamburgers, try kebabs made with cubed gammon and pineapple, fish and melon, king prawns and peppers, liver and kidney with mushrooms and courgettes. But the most popular accompaniments – jacket potatoes, green or rice salad or coleslaw, garlic or herb loaves in foil, and punchy sauces – are hard to beat.

67 | Cubes of meat packed tightly together on a skewer will result in tender, pink-centred kebabs. You have to separate the pieces for those who like theirs well done.

68 | Avoid the clutter of plates and knives. Kebabs are easily served with a portion of salad inside warm split-open pitta bread for simple eating with fingers.

69 | To tenderise meat or fish and impregnate it with extra flavour, make up marinades using red or white wine vinegar or lemon or lime juice, olive oil and ground pepper. Never add salt, as this draws out the juices, drying and therefore toughening the meat. Experiment with extra flavours when marinating. My own favourites are clear honey, soy sauce, garlic, ginger, peanut butter and Italian red or green pesto. Not all at once you understand, just as appropriate. But there must always be sufficient olive oil to coat and protect the food against air which can cause it to decompose.

Vegetables

In General

| 70 | Cook root veg with a lid on, greens without. You may remember this rule of thumb more easily if you think of underground vegetables being covered, above-ground varieties exposed. |

| 71 | Pop a small piece of fat or a teaspoon of oil in the water when cooking greens or potatoes, and they won't boil over. |

| 72 | Add lemon juice to the boiling water when cooking cauliflower, for snowy whiteness without a strong smell. Many cooks claim that a bay leaf added to the cauliflower cooking liquid keeps kitchen air fresh. When cooking other vegetables, dropping a piece of stale bread in the water absorbs smells. |

73 Old chefs' tips for banishing cabbage smells include adding a whole small onion, a stalk of celery or a couple of unshelled walnuts; these apparently do the trick without spoiling the taste of the cabbage. Adding a sprig of mint to boiling cabbage gives it an interesting flavour without the school-dinner aroma.

74 Cut the cost of cooking a variety of vegetables by steaming the fast-cooked varieties, such as Brussels sprouts, courgettes and leeks, over slower-cooking root vegetables – potatoes, carrots, swede etc.

75 Picky eaters, children and the sick or elderly will often find a puréed vegetable more appetising. Cooked sprouts or beetroot popped into a blender with butter or seasoning, or mashed combinations of root vegetables – carrots and swede, turnips and parsnip – are all delicious. Top with a sprinkling of sunflower seeds. This is also a good rescue remedy for over-cooked vegetables which are too soggy to serve whole.

76 │ Lining the bottom of the salad drawer with kitchen paper before storing vegetables, fruit and salad ingredients will keep them fresher longer.

77 │ Leftover vegetables can be chopped finely or puréed and added to soup. Or you can make a vegetable gratin. Fold whole vegetable pieces into a cheese sauce, top with a sprinkling of grated cheese and breadcrumbs, dot with butter and pop under a hot grill.

Legumes

78 │ By adding a pinch of bicarbonate of soda to water in which you soak dried beans and peas, they'll soften quicker, speeding up and saving money on the cooking. It's also an old ruse for restoring colour to older vegetables. Unfortunately, it does deplete the vitamin content, so should only be used as a last resort.

79 │ Never add salt to dried peas, beans etc. before the final stages of cooking, as this hardens the skin and turns them into bullets. Don't throw away inedible or old legumes. Drained and dried they can still be useful as 'weights' for baking pastry blind.

80 │ Although it is always advisable to soak dried beans before cooking, *over*-steeping – i.e. beyond 6-8 hours – leads to germination and fermentation which in turn causes indigestion. If you haven't pre-soaked, place dried beans in cold water, bring to the boil, drain and throw this water out; replace with fresh and repeat the process; third time round, bring to the boil and continue cooking until tender *(see 166)*.

Green Vegetables

81 It isn't necessary, let alone thrifty, to discard the hard core of cabbage. Shred it on the coarse side of your grater and add it to the chopped up remainder, or use it in soups or vegetable stock.

82 To get the maximum amount of nutrients and flavour from peas – fresh or frozen – cover the bottom of the pan with a layer of lettuce leaves. Place the peas on top of this without adding water. Another layer of lettuce on top and very slow cooking will give them all the moisture they need.

83 Cut a X with a sharp knife in the bottoms of vegetables such as cauliflower, broccoli and sprouts, where the stem is tougher than the head, for quick uniform cooking.

84 When cooking spinach, wash it well and cook in just the water adhering to the leaves. Watch carefully to prevent burning. 1lb (450g) fresh spinach would equal an 8oz (225g) frozen pack. 3lb (1.3kg) raw spinach will cook down to 1lb (450g) ready to serve. Don't use an aluminium or iron pan, or the spinach will have a metallic flavour. Raw young spinach leaves are colourful and tasty in a salad.

85 A dash of vinegar added to the washing water when preparing brassicas – sprouts, cauli and cabbage etc – will draw out any lurking creepy-crawlies and hidden dirt.

86 When planning to stuff cabbage leaves, make a note to put the cabbage in the freezer the day before. Thawed and cored when you're ready to cook, the leaves will separate easily.

87 | Cabbage and other vegetables which some find hard to digest won't have anti-social after-effects if the leaves are boiled for just a few minutes, drained and the water thrown away. Add a few caraway seeds to the vegetable and just enough fresh boiling water to cover. Return to the heat and continue to cook until tender.

88 | For free and nutritious vegetables pick and boil the tops from very young nettles and enjoy a taste not unlike spinach. Pinch out the tops of broad beans too. Picked and lightly boiled as soon as the pods start to appear they are eminently palatable.

Root and Other Vegetables

89 | Two carrots a day are better than an apple for health, according to the latest findings on foods which help prevent heart disease. Use young grated carrots in salads, slice them lengthways and sprinkle them with lemon juice and salt to accompany drinks or dips, and to keep as ready nibbles in the fridge for weight-watchers.

90 | Root vegetables – swedes, carrots and beetroot for example – will keep longer if placed in layers of clean, dry sand in boxes in a cool place. Fine ash or dry peat can be substituted for sand.

91 | Never store carrots with the leaves intact, as the green tops drain them of moisture. And never store them near apples, which impart a bitter taste to carrots. Jazz up geriatric carrots by adding sugar and butter and just enough lightly salted water to cover them in cooking. It gives them an attractive glaze and a greatly improved flavour.

92 Beetroot bleeds easily if bruised or cut and thus loses much of its colour and goodness when boiled. Rub the 'leaks' with salt to prevent this. Peel beetroot easily after cooking by first draining them then plunging into cold water. Whole beetroots baked in their skins are delicious!

93 Boil corn on the cob in unsalted water, as salt toughens the kernels. Add seasoning and butter afterwards. The corn is ready to eat when a milky, not watery, liquid comes out of the grains when pierced. A metal shoe horn is better than a knife for removing the kernels from the cob.

94 Celery will cook more quickly if cut diagonally rather than horizontally across the stalk. A toothbrush is the best implement for cleaning celery; a pot scourer works better on carrots.

95 Larger aubergines (eggplants) can have a bitter taste unless you 'degorge' them. Chop in chunks or slice and sprinkle with salt. Place in a colander and allow the salt to draw out the acrid liquid. Dry with kitchen paper before cooking. This helps restrict the amount of oil they normally guzzle up in cooking, but slimmers should dip them first in lightly beaten egg white as a protective coating before frying.

96 Artichokes should never be cooked in aluminium pans, or they'll turn an unappetising grey colour. A dash of lemon or vinegar enhances flavour and colour. Throw away artichoke leftovers: toxins caused by their iron content make storing them for more than a day inadvisable.

97 Mushrooms are often cheaper when bought in bulk, but
deteriorate quickly. They fade even faster in a plastic bag, but
will keep fresh for up to a week in a brown paper one. If
possible avoid washing them in water or removing the outer
skin to prevent them absorbing water and losing nutrients and
flavour. A wipe with kitchen paper is all that is needed for
prime mushrooms.

98 When you have a glut of mushrooms, dry them for later use.
Wipe over with a damp cloth, then dry in a warm oven until
completely dried out with no moisture remaining. Alternatively mushrooms can be frozen: mince or finely chop them,
add a little water or stock, and freeze.

99 Sauté mushrooms in butter with a little lemon juice to bring
out the flavour and avoid discoloration.

Tomatoes

| 100 | Ratatouille is an easy-to-cook, nutritious and mouth-watering way to serve vegetables, but can be expensive, especially when tomatoes are out of season. However tinned tomatoes are excellent in this dish – replace 1lb (450g) fresh tomatoes with a 14oz (400g) can. In the unlikely event of having enough left over for another day, ring the changes by reheating it with the addition of a finely chopped fresh chilli pepper.

| 101 | When using stronger tasting tinned, puréed or sun-dried tomatoes, add a pinch of sugar to counterbalance the acidity.

| 102 | Sun-dried tomatoes are a flavour-rich ingredient for any amount of dishes. By the time tomatoes are cheap and plentiful in the shops, the sun is usually past its strongest but you can dry them in the oven. Only ripe, unblemished tomatoes should be used. Preheat the oven to 225°F (110°C) Gas Mark ¼. Coarsely slice the tomatoes and spread them on racks on top of baking sheets. Add a little sprinkling of salt and bake for 4-7 hours. This is obviously only economical if you are doing a large quantity, or at the same time as other slow-cooking dishes. It's ideal in the cool oven of an Aga. When completely dry, store the tomato slices in jars, well-sealed greaseproof bags, or herb-flavoured oil *(see 171)*.

| 103 | Ripen green tomatoes by putting them in a dark place such as a drawer, wrapped in newspaper, with a ripe tomato or an apple for company. Or pop them in brown paper bags and leave them on a sunny windowsill; without the bag to filter the light, they would just soften rather than ripen. When a whole truss falls off a plant, hang it up near a light window in a warm kitchen and the tomatoes will gradually ripen on the stalks.

| 104 | When making a creamed tomato soup, avoid curdling by adding the cooked tomato ingredients to the milk or cream rather than the other way round. (Never re-boil a soup which has had milk or cream added.)

105   Get the last bit of tomato (or garlic) purée from the tubes by warming the tube for a few seconds in hot water before removing the cap. Squeeze out the last drop with a rolling pin.

Potatoes

106   Potatoes won't sprout if they are stored with a few apples in a cool corner.

107   Clean and peel potatoes inside a colander placed in a bowl of water for speed and tidiness. Just lift colander and peelings out.

108   An excess of peeled potatoes will keep for a few days in the fridge if a teaspoon of vinegar is added to their bowl of water. Raw peeled potatoes won't go brown if you pop a slice of bread or a piece of washed charcoal or coal in the water with them. Even new potatoes can be prepared well in advance by adding half a cup of milk to enough cold water to cover and setting them aside in a cool place.

109   Where time is of the essence, speed up the scraping of new potatoes by leaving them to soak in boiling water to which a pinch of bicarbonate of soda has been added, while you get on with something else. After about 5 minutes the skins will rub off easily.

110   Potatoes cut lengthways will cook more quickly than when cut across, and will be less inclined to go mushy.

111 Raw sliced potato will absorb excess salt from stews and other dishes. Taste and add the potato at the last stages of cooking. For over-salted soups, a grated potato can be added.

112 When shopping for potatoes, it's tempting to buy the varieties being offered at bargain prices, but it's worth remembering that Desirée is unbeatable for a crunchy-outer, floury-inner texture for roast, plain, boiled or mashed potatoes; Cara is best for perfect baked potatoes in their jackets; and Kerr's Pinks make sensational chips.

113 When possible, boil or bake potatoes in their skins, as peeling removes much of the Vitamin C content. Just scrub them, remove 'eyes' and any green parts and pop them in cold salted water to keep them fresh until cooking time.

114 For quick-bake potatoes, allow them to stand in hot water for 15 minutes first, or stick small skewers through the middle to conduct the heat. Always, prick with a fork to prevent the skins exploding with the build-up of heat, and rub them with oil and salt to ensure crispy jackets.

115 Revive leftover baked potatoes by putting them first in boiling water and then in a hot oven at 425°F (220°C) Gas Mark 7 for about 20 minutes.

116 You can use old potatoes for a potato salad if you boil them gently in their jackets until they are just ready. Remove from the heat and allow them to cool in their cooking water. When drained, the cold potato skins will slide off and the potatoes will be smooth and waxy for dicing.

117 It's important to add oil and vinegar dressing to potato salad while the potatoes are still hot – the potatoes will absorb the flavours – but mayonnaise-based dressings should only be added when the potatoes are cold.

118 For light and creamy mashed potatoes, heat the milk before adding it to the potatoes along with a knob of butter. A quick and economical trick is to put some of the potato water in a jug as you drain them, mix a little powdered milk with the water and return to the dry potatoes. Powdered milk is a useful standby for thickening over-runny creamed potato.

119 Improve the blandness of mashed potato by adding the beaten yolk of an egg when they've been drained and mashed. The whisked egg white folded in just before you serve will make them extra light and fluffy.

120 If you have more milk than you need, cook potatoes in it. Drain the milk and mash the potatoes with a knob of butter. Superb. Frugal cooks use up the drained milk in a cheese sauce.

121 If potatoes have been cooked ahead of the rest of the meal, mash them with butter then pour hot milk carefully on top. Keep the pan in a warm place and the potatoes will stay moist and heated through until required.

122 Quick, crispy roast potatoes are guaranteed by first choosing the right variety *(see 112)* and par-boiling them for 3-10 minutes depending on type. Drain them, put the lid back on the pan and give it a good shake up and down to roughen the outsides of the potatoes: this is quicker than scoring them with a fork. Roll the potatoes in seasoned flour then cook in lard, dripping or duck fat *(see 37)* in the highest part of the oven at 425°F (220°C) Gas Mark 7 for an hour or until brown.

123 For crisper, chipped potatoes, pour salted boiling water over the uncooked chips, drain them and dry them well before cooking. (*Always* dry potatoes before adding to hot fat to avoid splattering.) If potatoes seem slow to brown, remove them from the fat and allow the heat to come up to full again before carefully lowering the chips back into the fat. They will now crisp in seconds.

124 To make your own potato crisps, slice the peeled potato thinly using a potato peeler. Dry the slices well, and deep-fry in hot oil, shaking the pan occasionally to keep the crisps separated. Potato crisps can be frozen. Those left out, or soggy when bought or home-made, will crisp up if spread on a baking sheet and put in a fairly hot oven – 375°F (190°C) Gas Mark 5 – for a few minutes.

125 To absorb the fat from greasy chips, either place them on kitchen paper and sprinkle them with salt as they're taken from the pan, or shake them with salt in a large brown paper bag.

Onions

126   Peeling and chopping onions without crying could become the sole topic of a book, I feel, as there are so many tips to choose from. Hold a fork or spoon between clenched teeth (my favourite, it's so quick, however daft) or wear goggles, another loony but effective method. Many cooks swear by keeping them in the fridge in a sealed container, or popping them in the freezer for 15 minutes before you cut them to 'fix' the essential, tear-jerking oil. Then there's the one about peeling them under running cold water. The method most recommended for button onions is to place them in a pan and pour boiling water over them; drain and put them in a bowl, cover with cold water and peel straightaway.

127   Where shallots are called for rather than onions in a recipe, it's worth making the special purchase to get the flavour of the dish right. Shallots are nearer to garlic in flavour, and like garlic, burn easily, so take care not to let them brown or they taste bitter.

128   Browning onions can take forever. Instead of turning the heat up – which only turns them black, tough and acrid – add a little sugar to the frying pan for a nice golden brown in half the cooking time.

129   When baking whole onions, they'll stay whole if a X is cut into the base with a sharp knife. Coat smaller onions with flour to keep them intact during cooking.

130   Keep half-used onions (or green peppers) fresh for longer by storing them in screw-top jars in the refrigerator. (A bunch of parsley will stay fresh like this too – invert the jar.)

131 Keep an onion on top of a glass of water in the kitchen where it will soon sprout; the green tops can be snipped off and added to stews, soups and salads for flavouring. If you *don't* want onions to sprout, a smallish amount will keep best in a plastic container in the fridge.

132 Take advantage of cut-price onions by buying in bulk. They store well in the legs of old stockings and tights hung up in a cool place. Onions which sprout lose much of their goodness, so prevent this by first singeing the roots of each one with a red-hot poker before hanging.

133 The Chinese use spring onions in practically every dish to clear the body of impurities and, as they so delicately put it, to 'chase the wind'. As they are so very adaptable and easily digestible, it's a habit worth adopting. They're easily grown in a window box.

Garlic

134 Garlic is cheapest when you grow your own in a window box or garden. Bruise a few cloves of garlic gently before planting. The French, who should know, plant theirs in the second week of March to get one large round head of cloves and from October to February to produce several smaller heads.

135 Garlic bought in quantity has a tendency to dry out and shrink before you can use it all. Pop the peeled cloves in a jar of olive oil. Not only will they last for ages, but you can drain off the garlic-flavoured oil for cooking. (Top the jar up with more olive oil).

136 Sprinkle a little salt on a garlic clove so that it won't stick to the knife, chopping board or garlic press when being crushed or chopped.

137   To remove the smells of onion, garlic and other strong flavours from your hands, rub them with a little dried mustard powder, cold water and salt. Or rub fresh parsley vigorously into the skin to release the juice. Or rub your hands with a raw potato, lemon juice or vinegar.

138   To remove the smell of onions or garlic from a chopping board, rub it over with a cut lemon, salt or celery leaves.

139   Garlic won't leave such a strong aftertaste if you first remove the green or yellow centre shoot before crushing it. Otherwise, don't bother to skin garlic cloves, you'll only make your hands smell, and the insides will pop out easily through the skin in a garlic press. Or crush the clove lightly with the flat of a knife blade, and the skin will peel off easily.

140   For reasons of flavour and economy, it's worth remembering when cooking with garlic that 1 crushed clove equals 3 chopped.

141   When garlic and onion are fried in a recipe, always cook the onion first until hot and transparent before adding the garlic.

See also 474.

Salads and Salad Dressings

Salad Leaves

142 Dry washed salad leaves by shaking the surface water from them, then place them in the centre of a clean tea towel. Gathering the corners and sides together to keep them from flying around, whirl the towel with large circular arm movements above your head. For large quantities, pop the leaves in a clean pillowcase and, with the end well sealed, give it a few seconds on the spin-dry programme of your washing machine!

143 Keep lettuces fresh for at least a week by wrapping them – unwashed and untrimmed – in newspaper and storing them in a cool dark place.

144 Never use salt in the water when washing lettuce, as the leaves go limp. But a few drops of lemon juice crisp up lettuce nicely and drive out any clinging beasties.

145 Never cut lettuce leaves with a knife, as the edges will quickly collapse. Tear the leaves gently into pieces and pop into a plastic bag to remain crisp for half an hour or so while you prepare the rest of the meal.

146 Fresh watercress, inverted in a bowl of very cold water will stay fresh by absorbing moisture through its leaves. When watercress is wanted for a garnish, leave the rubber band on until the bunch has been washed and the surplus water shaken out. Then simply chop above the band to remove the coarse stems for quick and easy handling.

147 Never toss a green salad in vinaigrette until absolutely the last moment. Acid from the vinegar will make the lettuce collapse. But if you toss salad greens first with olive oil and then add vinegar or lemon juice the leaves will not wilt so quickly.

148 When you have added dressing to a salad and the taste is too vinegary for your liking, add a few cubes of bread. Lightly toss through to absorb some of the vinegary mix. Remove the bread, sprinkle a little olive oil over the dressing and toss again before serving. Slightly stale pitta bread, toasted or baked then broken up and added to a salad, is a palatable ingredient whether or not you've been heavy-handed with the dressing.

149 Dressed salad does not travel well. For picnics, prepare and pack salad leaves in a plastic bag. Keep the dressing separate in a screw-top jar. When needed, pour the dressing into the bag, seal it very firmly at the top and give it a shake to mix thoroughly.

150 Once salad has been drenched in dressing, it's virtually useless as leftovers unless you turn it quickly into a mock *gazpacho*. Pop all the salad remains into a blender with a pint of tomato juice and a few drops of Tabasco and whisk for a few seconds before serving with a garnish of croûtons, diced green peppers or cucumber.

151 To protect the surface of wooden salad bowls, treat with a thin coating of olive oil on kitchen paper. Rub with a cut clove of garlic before salad leaves are added. Never wash wooden bowls if possible, just clean with oil and a little salt on kitchen paper.

Other Salad Ingredients

|152| Radishes will stay crisp for days if placed leaves down in water with their roots in the air. To make radish 'flowers', top and tail them and with a sharp knife make six lengthways cuts keeping the base intact. Store in a bowl of cold water in the fridge for at least an hour, and the sections will open out like petals.

|153| Many salad vegetables will revive when soaked for a couple of minutes in ice-cold water – you can add ice cubes. Dry thoroughly and wrap the firmed-up veg loosely in a damp tea towel. Leave in the fridge for a few hours.

|154| The simplest way to keep celery fresh once it has been taken out of its plastic sleeve and trimmed, is to chop the bottoms square across and stand the stalks in a jug of chilled water.

|155| Celery can be made into pretty garnishing sprays by first chopping the stalk up into 3 inch (7.5cm) pieces. Now cut each section lengthways into fine strips keeping 1 inch (2.5cm) intact for a base. Pop into a bowl of cold water and leave in the fridge for a few hours until they fan out.

|156| The most economical way to buy olives is loose from a delicatessen. Keep them in the fridge with a slice of lemon on top. Dry shrivelled olives will plump out again if stored in a jar of olive oil in a cool pantry.

157 If you peel peppers, some of their taste is lost. But some recipes require the skin to be removed. To do this, place under a hot grill until the skins blacken and blister. Remove the peppers, place in cold water, and the skins will rub off easily.

158 If you don't like skins on salad tomatoes, pour boiling water over them and leave to stand in the water for a couple of minutes. They will peel easily. Always slice tomatoes lengthways – stalk end to base. They'll be firmer than slices cut across.

159 Test an avocado for ripeness by gently pressing the pointed end. This should easily yield to your thumb if ready to eat. Speed the ripening of avocados by leaving them in an airing cupboard or barely warm oven overnight. Sealing them in a brown paper bag will also soften them.

160 If you store avocados for too long in a fridge, they will have unappetising brown streaks in the flesh, although they're still fine to eat. The best way to keep them without discoloration is in flour in an earthenware container. An avocado develops brown spots when becoming overripe.

161 Special avocado dishes are unnecessary. Serve stable and wobble-free avocado halves by thinly slicing off the round bit from the bottom of each.

162 Cucumber becomes more digestible if it is cut lengthways, sprinkled with salt and lemon juice and left for a few hours in a cool place. Drain off the surplus liquid before serving.

163 To eke out a salad for unexpected guests, or to add colourful variety to an everyday salad, add frozen vegetables. Sweetcorn kernels, diced peppers and cauliflower florets etc. have already been blanched, and once thawed and coated in a salad dressing are ready to eat.

164 Green tips on chicory leaves are not a sign of freshness but of bitterness. so choose paler specimens. Do not try to revive limp chicory in bowls of ice water: the more it comes in contact with water, the more pungent it becomes.

165 Those large plastic sweet jars with drainage holes pierced in the bottom, make ideal containers for growing your own beansprouts. Scald with boiling water between batches to kill bacteria. Beans can produce up to six times their volume, so 2 tablespoons are ample to allow room to expand. First soak the beans overnight in cold water. Next morning drain the liquid and give it to your houseplants. Rinse the beans and put them in the jar. Cover the top with muslin or a clean white handkerchief held taut with an elastic band. Leave in the airing cupboard or other warm corner. Water daily by pouring water through the muslin top and allowing it to drain out of the bottom, thus disturbing the beans as little as possible. In less than a week you should have healthy sprouts. Cress and alfalfa seeds grow quickly on wet blotting paper.

166 Red kidney and butter (lima) beans are delicious in salads. They can contain toxic substances but are perfectly safe to eat providing they are boiled hard for a minimum of 10 minutes in a pan without a lid. After that the heat can be lowered and the beans allowed to continue cooking at a simmering level until tender *(see 78-80)*.

Salad Dressings

167 A baby's feeding bottle is the ideal container for making salad dressing in, as it helps you measure the right proportions of oil and vinegar. As a general guide, it's three parts oil to one of vinegar. First dissolve any flavours or seasonings – sugar, mustard, salt, pepper – in the vinegar first, then having shaken them vigorously, add the oil and shake again. To save time keep a generous amount ready made up in a cool dark place.

168 Use only olive oil and not, despite its description, salad oil for vinaigrette. Virgin and extra virgin olive oil, are the purest, strongest flavoured and, say latest reports, the healthiest types of oil. If you find the taste too strong and the price prohibitive, experiment with the medium-priced range, where flavours are still very acceptable. Find your favourite and stick to it, as it will pay you to buy in quantity when you use it to cook every day.

169   Always decant olive oil from a plastic bottle to a glass one after it's been opened, as it will store better. Keep in a cool place and out of light which is harmful to olive oil. A dark green, well-stoppered wine bottle makes an ideal container.

170   Olive oil does not improve with age, and if you are worried that it will spoil, you can store it in the fridge, This won't affect the flavour, but will make it cloudy. However, once restored to room temperature, the colour will return to normal. Placing the bottle under a warm tap or standing it in a jug of warm water will accelerate the process.

171   Herb-flavoured oil is a useful addition to any amount of dishes, from mayonnaise to barbecue marinades. Select only prime fresh herb leaves and stems. Use a 12fl oz (350ml) bottle with a tightly fitting lid. Place the herbs in the bottle and fill with olive oil. Close tightly and store in a cool dark place for not less than 3 weeks. Now strain into another jar or bottle, adding a few fresh sprigs of the same herb to decorate and accentuate the taste. It's now ready to use. Keep tightly capped in the refrigerator.

172   White wine left over at the end of the bottle can be added to vinegar to be used in dressings. Or add a few drops of olive oil to opened red or white wine which you intend to use in cooking – it will keep for much longer.

Flavourings

Condiments

173 Keep a kitchen shaker handy containing six parts salt to one part ground pepper so that you always have instant seasoning ready.

174 White pepper pots won't have clogged holes if you place a dried pea in with the pepper. But by doing away with powdered pepper altogether, and only using freshly ground peppercorns, you will add instant 'spice' to your culinary life. Similarly, coarse, rock salt or sea salt will improve the flavour of food enormously.

175 Salt pots run freely if a few grains of uncooked rice are placed in with the salt. Wooden or stoneware containers are better than glass as they absorb any moisture; you can improve matters by lining the bottom of the pot with blotting paper.

176 They say Mr Colman made his fortune from the mustard people throw away. Save on powdered mustard by adding a pinch of salt as you mix it with water, oil, beer or milk (depending on the flavour you want). This will stop the hardening and drying-out process.

177 Adding a teaspoon of made mustard brings out the full flavour of a cheese sauce.

Herbs

178 If a recipe gives quantities for fresh herbs and you have only dried, use just half the amount suggested, as dried herbs are much more concentrated than fresh. Dried herbs lose their aroma quickly. Test with your nose. If they seem 'fusty', throw them away (or sprinkle over the soil of your house plants to give them a little extra 'food').

See also 60.

179 When you have a bumper crop of fresh herbs, pick them when young and green and dry them for winter. Place them on baking sheets in a very cool oven and leave them until they are dry enough to be rubbed into small pieces. It's also easy to make your own celery 'flakes' for adding to savoury dishes and soups. Just chop and wash celery leaves after removing them from the stalks, dry on a baking tray in a low oven, crumble when bone dry and store in labelled airtight jars.

180 Use marigold petals to colour food instead of wildly expensive saffron. Light and delicate in flavour, they are easy to dry and store. Place in a cool dark place in thin layers to dry out slowly and preserve their rich colour.

181 It's easy and economical to grow herbs in pots and window boxes if you don't have a garden. Mint in fact *needs* a container – because of its invasive roots, but preferably not a window box or it will quickly obscure the view and choke everything around it. Parsley can be difficult to germinate unless you pour boiling water on the seeds and allow them to soak for 24 hours before putting them in compost. Supermarkets and green-grocers have now cottoned on to selling fresh herbs in tubs rather than as scrawny bunches in warm plastic bags and you can keep them for some time on a kitchen window-sill or plant them out.

182 Many fresh herbs can be frozen. If you have more than you can use at one time, chop and freeze the surplus amount in ice cube trays topped up with water. Transfer to freezer bags when frozen. Add to soups, casseroles and sauces. Parsley can be frozen in bunches in bags and stored in the freezer after thoroughly washing and drying. Before defrosting, smash the parsley up while it's still inside the bag and shake out the required amount.

183 To preserve the vivid green colour of parsley before drying, hold the bunch by the stems and dip it into boiling water. Shake off the surplus moisture or dry on kitchen paper before drying in a low oven.

184 For a decorative and tasty accompaniment to deep-fried fish, wash and dry 6-7 sprays of parsley. After taking the cooked fish our of the deep-fat fryer, put the parsley sprigs into the basket and turn off the heat. Lower the basket gently into the hot fat and fry for 1-2 minutes. Place on kitchen paper to absorb the grease.

185 Rather than buying those overpriced tea-bag things, make your own *bouquet garni* from parsley stalks, 2 sprigs of thyme and a bay leaf tied in a small piece of muslin. (Buy a roll of broad white bandage and cut up as required.)

186 Basil, which is easy to grow on a kitchen window-sill, and mint, which isn't (but a tub at the back door is ideal), are excellent fly repellents for the pantry or kitchen in summer.

187 Keep bay leaves fresh in an airtight jar with a piece of cotton wool laced with olive oil for company.

Spices

188 Buy commercial ground spices in small quantities only, as they lose their flavours very quickly. It's best to buy spices whole and grind them yourself (in a mortar, a spice grinder or coffee grinder).

189 Preserve fresh ginger in a jar of vodka.

Fruit and Nuts

Dried Fruit

190 It's not just the high dietary fibre in prunes which accounts for the fact that we eat twice as many now as we did 5 years ago. They contain virtually no fat but are a good source of iron, which makes them ideal for slimmers. Soak prunes in strong Indian tea until they plump up. You don't have to throw the tea away, you can cook the prunes in it. Other dried fruits can be soaked in the same way: try China tea for a change, it's particularly good with apricots, figs etc.

191 A quick and economical way to stew prunes for breakfast is to heat a vacuum flask with hot water, toss the water away and add the prunes. Top up with boiling water or tea, screw the top on and leave overnight.

192 Dip the chopping knife in cold water first and dates won't stick to it. To skin dates, remove stalks, squeeze the end and a naked date will emerge. Whole dates, stoned and chopped, are cheaper and as tasty as mixed dried fruit for cakes, puddings, scones and biscuits.

Apples and Other Fruit

193 In the autumn, when fruit such as plums, apples and pears are plentiful, buy in bulk for the freezer. They freeze best if cooked lightly in sugar syrup.

194 If you give your home-grown apples a rub over with a cloth dipped in glycerine before storing them away, stalk end up, in a cool damp-free corner, they should keep all winter.

195 An apple placed with underripe tomatoes, peaches, plums, pears etc. will cause them to ripen quicker. So keep apples separately if you *don't* want this to happen.

196 For best results when stewing apples, add a dash of lemon juice to preserve the colour and release the flavour. Add sugar and a knob of butter in the later stages of cooking.

197 Overripe fruit can be puréed with sugar and a dash of lemon juice. When folded into whipped cream it re-emerges as a scrumptious fruit fool.

198 Adding a couple of teaspoons of arrowroot or cornflour to the sugar when making a fruit pie will thicken the juices, preventing leakage.

199 To stop bananas and other fruit which discolour quickly from going brown as you prepare a fruit salad, sprinkle with lemon juice.

200 The fridge is the least suitable place for keeping bananas, but oddly enough, you can freeze them when they become over-ripe. Add a little lemon juice as you mash them, and pack in small tubs to use later in bread and cake recipes.

201 Slimmers tend to avoid bananas because of their high calorie count, despite the fact that they have many energy-boosting and nutritious qualities. They are at their most calorific when unripe; the starch content decreases as they ripen. Non-slimmers might like to try bananas sprinkled with brown sugar and lemon juice, dotted with butter, rolled in kitchen foil parcels and cooked on the dying heat at the end of a barbecue. Serve with cream. Scrumptious.

202 Melons should be wrapped before putting them in the fridge to contain their smell. Overchilled melons will lose their flavour, so only chill briefly before serving. To test if a melon is ripe, press the stalk end gently; it should give a little and release its distinctive smell.

203 Fresh pineapple is mouth-watering but a pain to peel and core. Apple corers, small round pastry cutters or the sharp end of a cigar tube can cut out the core when the fruit is sliced. Pineapple is good for the digestion, so makes an ideal end to a rich meal. Sprinkling it with Kirsch is a popular way to serve it as a pudding; sprinkling it with salt draws out much of the acid content.

204 Cooking rhubarb in cold tea reduces its acidity. So too does steeping it in cold water to which a pinch of baking powder (bicarbonate of soda) has been added. Pre-soak for about 40 minutes before cooking and drain off the dark juice which this produces. Because of its high acid content, like spinach it should never be cooked in an aluminium pan or the taste will be spoiled.

205 Coconuts crack more easily if put in the oven at 300°F (150°C) Gas Mark 2 for 30 minutes, but you should first bore into the 'eyes' with a nail to remove the milk. They will most likely crack voluntarily as they cool; if not persuade them with a gentle tap from a hammer.

206 Add some of the coconut milk to the peeled and broken pieces of flesh to speedily shred them in a blender. Ordinary warm milk poured over elderly desiccated coconut will moisten it for use in curry dishes, cakes and biscuits, baking etc.

207 Save the juice of tinned fruit and freeze it in ice-cube trays. It's useful for adding to soft drinks or, when thawed, the cubes provide the small amounts needed for trifle bases or fresh fruit salad.

Soft Summer Fruits

208 When cheap and plentiful, buy raspberries, gooseberries, cherries, grapes, red and black currants, and blackberries. After removing the stalks and washing if necessary, place them dry on trays in the freezer, well spread out so they freeze separately. Once frozen they are easily handled – like boiled sweets – for decanting into plastic tubs or bags.

209 Black (or red) currants are quick to prepare after picking if a fork is used to strip them from their stalks. But don't even bother to do this if freezing. Freeze as above (208), then pack them in plastic tubs. When they're needed, a vigorous shake in the container will separate berries and stalks. If growing your own blackberries or looking for a healthy variety for jam-making, 'Baldwin' has the highest Vitamin C content.

210 The fuzzy skin on peaches which sets teeth on edge, can be quickly removed. Cover the fruit with boiling water for 10 seconds.

211 Sharp nail scissors are perfect for topping and tailing goose-berries, but don't bother if freezing, as they'll break themselves off.

212 Peel grapes as you would tomatoes – put them in a colander and lower them into boiling water, or pour it over them in a bowl. Leave for a minute before peeling.

213 I have heard many wonderful suggestions for enriching the flavour of strawberries. They range from sprinkling with lemon juice – of course – to tossing in a little wine vinegar or marinating in red wine or orange juice. A friend always adds freshly ground black pepper before serving, and they really do taste rather good.

214 Washing your hands with warm soapy water after picking or preparing cherries will only help to set the stain. Wipe hands with vinegar first and the stains will wash off easily.

Citrus Fruits

215 When buying citrus fruit, hold each piece in your hand and judge their value by weight rather than size. Light fruit will be full of pith or dried out; those full of juice and thin of skin will be heavier.

216 Don't discard grapefruit which have brown marks on their skins. Despite their dubious appearance, they are usually the best. Popping whole grapefruit in boiling water for a couple of minutes will separate segments from pith and make them easier to peel.

217 You can serve ice cream or sorbet attractively in whole, scooped out orange or lemon skins for individual portions. (A melon with its seeds and flesh scooped out is ideal for serving a larger amount.) The empty skins (with their caps for added decoration) will freeze, so can be prepared in advance.

218 To keep lemons fresh, store them in a jar of cold water, changing daily. Where you have an abundance of them, put a layer of sand an inch (2.5cm) deep in an earthenware pan. Place the lemons, without touching each other and stalk end downwards in the sand. Cover with more sand, and then arrange other layers in the same way until the pan is full. The sand should of course be clean, dry, builder's sand, but it's worth obtaining some as it will keep lemons for months in a cool place.

219 Keep a half lemon fresh by rubbing the cut surface with salt or vinegar and placing it, cut side down, on a saucer in the fridge.

220 Pieces of lemon can be sliced and frozen in a plastic container in the fridge, to use up at a later date. You could also make up ice cubes with slivers of lemon or orange already in them, handy when preparing cold drinks. Leftover freshly squeezed lemon or orange juice can also be frozen in cubes for another time. Keep unused lemon and orange rinds to form a freezer collection. It's wasteful to dry up a whole lemon when only some grated rind is called for, and frozen whole or part lemons are much easier to grate.

221 When you seriously mean lemon to be squeezed on food, do serve it in generous wedges rather than fiddly slices. Apart from enhancing the flavour of many dishes, the health-giving properties of lemons are legendary. Excellent for the liver and aiding digestion, they kill harmful bacteria on food as hot-country cooks who use them liberally can tell you.

222 To get the maximum amount of juice from a lemon (orange or grapefruit), warm it slightly in the oven, or pop it into boiling water or the microwave for a few seconds. Even rolling it in the warmth of your palms will noticeably increase the yield.

223 Where only a squirt of lemon juice is needed, don't cut into the lemon and have the rest curl up and die. Drop the lemon into boiling water to heat it, then stick a knitting needle, cocktail stick or fork into it and squeeze. Wrap the lemon in tin foil and it will keep fresh in the fridge.

224 Grating orange and lemon peel can be messy and wasteful unless the grater has first been run under the cold tap to make it non-stick. (The same applies to grating cheese.) Where it hasn't worked, use a pastry brush to remove the stubborn pieces.

225 You can absorb the tangy flavour needed for lemon or orange puddings by rubbing lump sugar over the skin to remove the oils.

The proper gadget for paring lemon and other citrus fruit rinds is a zester. It not only produces decorative thin coils of rind, it ensures that only the coloured part of the skin is removed, where the oil and desirable flavours are stored. The pith imparts a bitter flavour, so if using a grater, go lightly. A potato peeler makes a good stand-in zester.

 If you don't have an immediate use for fresh pared citrus rinds, place the thin strips on kitchen paper to absorb moisture overnight in a warm place. The dried peel can then be stored for future use.

Nuts

 Nuts won't go fusty or rancid if kept in a tightly sealed container in the fridge.

 Ordinary common or garden peanuts, plain or salted, can be made to taste like those spicy, pricey ones from delicatessens. Heat a knob of butter in a pan until frothy, add 2 teaspoons of curry powder and cook for a minute. Add a large packet of nuts and fry them in the curry mix for a further 2 minutes. Drain them on a piece of kitchen paper, and leave to cool.

 To quickly toast and skin shelled hazelnuts, spread them on a baking sheet and place in a moderate oven for 15 minutes or until the skins are brittle. Tip them out on to a clean cloth and run a rolling pin briskly over them to break up the outer skins. Rubbing the nuts in your hands can also help remove the skins.

231 Pop Brazils in a bag in the freezer for an hour or two before shelling. Or place them in a pan of cold water, bring them to the boil and after a minute, plunge them back into the cold. They'll shell easily with their contents still intact.

Soak pecan nuts overnight in cold water. When the shells are cracked, the kernels can be removed intact.

Soak walnuts in shells overnight in salty water. They'll crack easily without smashing the contents.

232 As with eggs, there is a 'floating in water' test for chestnuts and walnuts to find out if they are worth keeping. If the kernels inside are whole, they obviously weigh heavily and the nuts will sink to the bottom of a bowl of water. The nuts containing kernels which have shrivelled and dried will float.

233 Make a small slit in the skins of chestnuts before grilling or roasting to stop them exploding.

Eggs

In General

234 Brown eggs are no better than white eggs nutritionally; the colour of the egg is, with few exceptions, determined by the colour of the hen. But because consumers prefer brown eggs, suppliers often cash in and charge more for them. Don't fall for this con trick.

235 Pour salt on accidentally spilled raw egg before trying to mop it up. It will absorb the moisture and make the job much easier.

236 When an egg or eggs have stuck in their cardboard carton, remove all the non-stuck ones and soak the carton in water until it releases the captive eggs.

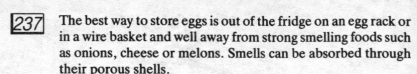

237   The best way to store eggs is out of the fridge on an egg rack or in a wire basket and well away from strong smelling foods such as onions, cheese or melons. Smells can be absorbed through their porous shells.

238   If you have more newly laid eggs than you can use, you can seal in the farm freshness by rubbing the shell over with glycerine on a clean cloth.

239   When putting all your eggs in one basket, mark with a X the ones to be used up first.

240   The odd egg white can be frozen into an ice cube and thawed out in the fridge up to 6 months later.

241   Egg whites will keep for several days in the fridge without going off. They will in fact beat better as they get older. The problem comes when you bring them out to use and can't remember how many are there. Weigh them and calculate one egg white per ounce (25g).

242   Leftover egg yolks dropped in a bowl of cold water and stored in a cool place will keep for several days.

243 Test eggs for freshness in a bowl of cold water. If they rise to the top they are unusable. If they tip on one end use them up fairly quickly, but if they lie on their sides at the bottom of the bowl they are fresh. Air gets into stale eggs making them lighter.

244 A fresh egg should keep a firm set white when broken into a frying pan; only older eggs run all over the place. Very fresh eggs take a little longer to cook.

See also 300-306, 391.

Boiling Eggs

245 When taking eggs from the fridge, cover them with cold water and bring to the boil. Plunging cold eggs into boiling water is a sure way to crack them.

246   Pierce an egg shell with a clean pin or needle before putting it in boiling water and it won't crack. A safety pin, or a headless matchstick broken in two and added to the water will also stop eggs cracking.

247   The easiest and cheapest way to ensure medium boiled eggs with soft yolks, nicely set whites and uncracked shells is to lower then gently into simmering water and cook for just 1 minute. Remove the pan from the heat but leave the eggs in with a lid on for 6 minutes and they'll be perfect.

248   When you want to hard-boil eggs, you need to start with cold water, bring it to the boil and time from then for another 7 minutes. They'll be thoroughly cooked without ending up like rubber bullets or with equally unappetising cold soft centres. Give hard-boiling eggs an occasional gentle stir with a wooden spoon to assist the uniform cooking of yolk and white.

249   Hard-boiled eggs can be difficult to shell without bits of the white adhering. Adding a spoonful of vinegar while boiling, and cracking the shell at each end after they've been removed from the boiling water and plunged into cold, will remedy this.

250   Parcel up a newly cracked egg in kitchen foil and it can still be gently boiled. Adding vinegar or lemon juice to the water as it simmers is the alternative.

251   When boiled eggs are taken from the heat, a sharp tap with a spoon at the pointed end will stop them cooking further.

252   Hard-boiled eggs plunged into cold water as soon as they're taken off the boil won't become discoloured around the yolks.

253 | If you pre-cook hard-boiled eggs, then can't tell them from raw later, twirl them on a flat surface: a raw one will spin, a cooked one won't.

254 | When hard-boiling eggs for Easter, add onion skins to the water and the eggs will emerge a rich golden brown. For purple eggs try beetroot juice, and for green try spinach water.

Poaching Eggs

255 | No need for a special poaching pan to poach eggs. Bring water to the boil in any saucepan and turn the heat off. Swirl the water vigorously with a spoon and gently break the egg in the middle to keep it from spreading. Put the lid on for a couple of minutes and the egg will poach gently in the hot water without becoming rubbery.

See also 256 and 257.

256 | Poached eggs will keep their shape in cooking if a teaspoon of vinegar is added to the boiling water. It also helps to break each egg into a saucer first before sliding it into the pan. Never use salt instead of vinegar, or it will break up the egg white and separate it from the yolk.

257 | An alternative way of poaching an egg is to place a small knob of butter in a cup and stand the cup in about an inch (2.5cm) of boiling water in a pan. Now break the egg into the cup, put the pan lid on and allow the egg to steam *off the heat* for about 7 minutes.

Scrambled Eggs and Omelettes

258 | Rinse a mixing bowl in cold water before beating eggs in it, and they won't stick to the sides.

259 Scrambled eggs are less likely to stick to the pan if the butter is melted thoroughly and swirled round the bottom and sides to coat the pan before the eggs are added.

260 A dash of bicarbonate of soda added to beaten egg when preparing an omelette will give it a much lighter, fluffier texture.

261 To make an omelette pan non-stick, heat the pan well before using, then scour it out with salt on a piece of greaseproof paper. Always make sure the butter is smoking hot before adding the eggs to the pan. An omelette pan must have a heavy metal bottom, and should only be used for omelettes or pancakes.

262 As eggs continue to cook off the heat, scrambled eggs and omelettes should be removed from the heat source before they are thoroughly cooked through. Rectify the disaster of having overcooked scrambled eggs to a rubbery mess, by stirring a raw beaten egg into them while they're still hot, and turning out onto a warm serving dish.

Dairy Foods

Milk

263 Fresh milk can be stored in the freezer. Put the cartons inside a freezer bag, or decant the milk into a larger container (to allow for expansion). When the milk has thawed out, just give it a really good shake.

264 Milk will keep fresh out of the fridge if decanted into a screw-top bottle inside a sleeve made from an old blanket. The material must first be soaked in cold water and it must cover the whole bottle. Keep in the shade out of doors, or in a cool pantry. Wet newspaper can form a makeshift bottle cover, but never let the paper dry out.

265 To stop milk sticking when heated, first put cold water in the pan. Swirl it round and empty it out before adding the milk.

266 | If milk is about to boil over, quickly remove it from the heat and give the pan a sharp knock as you put it down.

267 | To prevent milk boiling over, place a pie funnel in the centre of a saucepan. When the milk boils, it will shoot up the funnel and then fall back again without splashing over the sides of the pan.

268 | Never throw out milk which is 'on the turn'. Scones made with soured milk have a lovely light texture.

269 | If a recipe calls for sour milk and you haven't got any, stir a little lemon juice into ordinary milk and leave it for about half an hour at room temperature. It will become 'sour'.

270 | Buy dried skimmed milk for the store-cupboard and use it instead of fresh whenever you can in cooking. It's ideal for sauces, custards etc., and much cheaper and healthier because of its lower fat content.

Cream

271 | Cream beats better if the bowl, whisk and cream are all thoroughly chilled. To lessen the risk of overbeating cream, add sugar to it before you whip it.

272 | If natural yoghurt or a whipped egg white are folded into whipped double cream, the expensive cream will go further and be less fattening.

273 If a dish has been overseasoned, add some cream or natural yoghurt to it. This will 'flatten' the flavours. *(See also 111.)*

274 Whipped cream can be recycled by piping it or dropping it by the spoonful on to kitchen foil and freezing it. Store the pieces in freezer bags for garnishing cakes, puddings or coffee later. Alternatively, you can freeze whipped cream on kitchen foil in a cake tin to make a round and when set, pop it in a freezer bag. Defrost it ready to sandwich a sponge cake.

275 You can substitute equal quantities of single and double cream for whipping cream.

276 Whipped cream which has gone watery may be rectified by folding in an egg white; chill it thoroughly and when re-beaten it will fluff up again. Or carefully stir in some single or unwhipped double cream.

277 If cream (or milk) is beginning to go off, add a pinch of bicarbonate of soda. It gets rid of the sour taste, and halts the curdling process.

Butter

278 Before you cream butter, rinse the bowl in boiling water and dry quickly. The butter will now cream more easily. A cold slab of butter can be grated on the coarse side of the grater or cut into strips with a potato peeler to make it soften more speedily.

279 To make hard butter soft for quick spreading, and to make it go further, add a little boiling water. Beat it in drop by drop. Each 2oz (50g) of butter will absorb 1 teaspoon of water. Do this with margarine to produce a low-calorie spread for slimmers. Non-slimmers might prefer beating warm milk into the butter.

280 Before putting butter on the table in cold weather, rinse a basin with hot water and without drying it, cover the butter with it. The steam softens the butter without melting it.

281 If you haven't access to a fridge, keep butter fresh by placing it – still in its greaseproof wrapper – under fresh lettuce or cabbage leaves; sprinkle these liberally with salt. Or, still wrapped, place the butter in a bowl of very cold, well-salted water. Or wrap it in a cloth wrung out in vinegar and water, and keep underneath an inverted clay flowerpot.

282 To serve butter in clean-cut cubes, cut with dental floss rather than a knife. (You can cut fruit cake this way too.)

283 Soak rancid butter for 2-3 hours in cold water with a teaspoon of bicarbonate of soda, and you'll be able to eat it again. Or, for those partial to my more bizarre tips, stick a carrot in it overnight.

Yoghurt

284 When dishes call for cream, more and more health-conscious cooks are substituting natural yoghurt. Soured cream has 445 calories per cup, but even whole-milk yoghurt has only 165.

285 Put a whisked egg into natural yoghurt when using it in cooking and it won't separate. Or beat the yoghurt with a little cornflour to bind, and add it, a little at a time, to the dish being prepared.

286 Add yoghurt to curry or other hot spicy dishes to cool them down and make them easier to digest.

287 When you haven't time to cook, but need a healthy breakfast to start the day, add 1-2oz (25-50g) sultanas to a small 5oz (150g) natural yoghurt and leave in the fridge overnight for the sultanas to swell. This wholesome DIY yoghurt can also be used in cheesecake. Half and half milk and yoghurt whisked or popped in the blender for a few seconds makes a delicious and nourishing milk shake.

288   Save pounds by making your own yoghurt. I prefer the Greek style. To guarantee best results, use only a good quality, really fresh yoghurt as the starter.

> *2 level tablespoons skimmed milk powder*
> *18fl oz (550ml) fresh skimmed milk*
> *1 tablespoon prime, fresh Greek yoghurt*

Combine the powdered and fresh milk in a heavy pan, and simmer for 5 minutes. Remove from the heat and transfer to a bowl where it should be allowed to cool to just above lukewarm, or until you can comfortably dip a finger in it. Stir in the yoghurt. Pour the warm mix into a casserole dish with a lid, wrap it in a blanket and keep it in a warm place (the airing cupboard, for instance) for 5-6 hours. When set, pour off the liquid whey and pour the rest into a sieve lined with layers of kitchen paper so that it drips through into a bowl. Leave for 30 minutes to thicken. Cover the bowl and chill in the fridge. You can take a tablespoon from this to start your next batch.

Don't try to spoon it out before chilling or it will separate, and don't go on 'cooking' yoghurt after it's set – that will spoil it too.

Fold in flavourings and other ingredients after the yoghurt has finally set. Honey, maple syrup, puréed fruit, chopped dried fruit and nuts are all ideal.

A smaller quantity of yoghurt can be made in a wide-necked thermos flask. Put the cap on and leave it to set (3-5 hours). Unscrew the lid and place in the fridge to cool.

Cheese

289   Cheese should be kept in a cool pantry rather than the fridge as overchilling spoils the flavour. It won't go mouldy if you wrap it in muslin and sprinkle it with vinegar, or keep a lump of sugar on top. Either way, keep in a covered dish.

290   To stop cheese hardening, smear a film of butter around the exposed edges. Really dried-up old bits of cheese can be coarsely grated and frozen, ready to add to sauces at some later date. Kitchen foil is better than cling film for wrapping cheese.

291   Dried-out cheese will regain its moisture if soaked in butter-milk. An acceptable substitute is $1/2$ pint (300ml) milk with a teaspoon of bicarbonate of soda added to it.

292   Bland, mild, hard cheeses are usually cheaper and therefore tend to be bought 'just for cooking'. But in fact, because they have less flavour, you will need to use more than you would of the mature, full-flavoured kind. So a full-flavoured mature cheese can work out cheaper – especially if you can find end cuts at bargain prices.

293   Cheese should only be added to sauces after the basic sauce has been boiled through to cook it thoroughly. Stir in the cheese over sufficient heat to melt it but not enough to boil, which would make it tough and stringy.

294   A whole Stilton cheese will dry out quickly if you turn it into a crater by scooping out the centre. The best way is to slice whole rounds from the top and then cut these into individual wedges.

295   Look out for cut-price Stilton, Danish blue or similar cheeses which are often greatly reduced in price after Christmas, and keep them in the freezer. Grate and mix with the same weight of butter or margarine, mash well with a fork to soften, and serve in pots with crusty bread, or use as a sandwich filling, or to fill the hollows of celery sticks which are then chilled and cut into bite-sized pieces to serve when entertaining.

Sauce Making

White Sauces and Variations

 I was taught to make a basic béchamel or white sauce by allowing the flour and butter to cook well together before adding warmed milk – in generous splashes to allow the roux to expand – and stirring constantly until I had a smooth sauce. I still like this method. My teenage daughter, on the other hand, bungs butter, flour and cold milk in together and in a jiffy, agitating with a balloon whisk over a medium heat, gets a lump-free smooth sauce every time! Either method needs 1½ oz (40g) butter, 1oz (25g) flour, 15fl oz (450ml) liquid, and a cooking time, once it starts to bubble, of about 5-6 minutes. A teaspoon of cream stirred in at the last minute before serving gives a white sauce a nice glossy appearance.

297 A quick and flavourful white sauce can be made by gently frying chopped onion and celery in butter before stirring in the flour and continuing as above *(see 296)*.

298 Once a white sauce is cooked, and flavourings such as chopped parsley, mushrooms, cheese etc. are added, you can keep it warm until ready to serve by standing the sauce boat or jug in a saucepan of very hot water. Exclude the air which causes a skin to form on top by covering the surface with cling film or greaseproof paper. Or pour a little cold milk on the surface.

299 Any leftover white sauce or variation can be kept for a few days in the fridge. Put a knob of butter on the end of a fork and rub it over the surface while the sauce is still warm. Once refrigerated this will form a seal and stop a skin forming.

Egg-Based Sauces

300 Supercooks partial to egg-based sauces strain the whole beaten raw eggs before adding them to sauces or custards. It's wise for them to invest in an asbestos mat; when placed between the source of heat and bottom of the pan, this lessens the chances of egg sauces curdling.

301 To separate an egg yolk from the white, break the egg into a saucer, place a small upturned wine glass over the yolk and pour off the white.

302 To rescue a curdled hollandaise sauce, put a tablespoon of hot vinegar in a warm bowl and pour the separated sauce drop by drop into it until the whole amount is stirred in. Or mix 2 teaspoons of melted butter into an egg yolk. Stir this into the wayward sauce, follow with a tablespoon or two of hot water, and stir some more.

303 When Béarnaise sauce starts to separate, it can often be rescued by adding 1 teaspoon lukewarm water per 2 egg yolks. Beat rapidly until re-emulsified.

304 If home-made mayonnaise separates, start again using one or two egg yolks whisked until thick, then gradually add the curdled mayonnaise drop by drop. Or put a teaspoon of made mustard into a warm bowl and add the curdled mayonnaise to it, a tablespoon at a time, beating thoroughly between each one.

305 Having all the required ingredients for home-made mayonnaise at room temperature will lessen the chances of failure.

306 Fail-safe blender mayonnaise requires patience, 2 egg yolks, a tablespoon of wine vinegar or lemon juice, and a $1/2$ teaspoon each of dry mustard powder and salt. Blend to mix thoroughly, then slowly, in the thinnest trickle, beat in around $1/2$ pint (300ml) olive oil. Switch off as soon as the right consistency is reached. It will keep for 3 weeks in the refrigerator.

See also 391-2.

Pasta, Rice and Cereals

Pasta

307 Pasta should never really be cooked in advance – in theory – but in practice it's sometimes necessary. The best way to keep it hot without congealing is to first drain it and toss it in a little oil or butter, then keep it in a colander over a pan containing an inch or so of boiling water. Put a damp cloth over the colander.

308 Impecunious cooks mindful of saving on fuel bills, and others wanting perfectly cooked pasta, put it in boiling water and bring it back to the boiling point. They then turn off the heat and cover the pan with a tea-towel with a lid on top of that. In 15 minutes the pasta should have cooked itself, without *over*cooking.

309 Pasta, noodles and other starchy dishes won't boil over if you remember to rub the inside of the pan with vegetable oil first. Cook without a lid, unless you have condensation problems.

310 Add a generous tablespoon of oil to the salted water in which you cook pasta or noodles. It stops it sticking together during the cooking process. Stirring strands occasionally with a fork, to keep them on the move, also helps.

311 Italian chefs apparently chuck a strand of pasta against the wall to test if it's cooked; if it sticks it is ready. Fortunately, for those with insufficient time to wash the walls every time they have pasta, there is another method. Pasta is ready when you can just hold a piece between your teeth before biting into it, or *al dente* as they say in culinary circles. Timing therefore is crucial. A minute after *al dente* comes *all mushy*.

312 To revive leftover, undressed pasta, drop it in boiling water for a minute or so to heat through.

313 It's pointless to rinse cooked noodles in cold water, it really just succeeds in washing out the taste.

314 Add a couple of drops of yellow food colouring to packet noodles and pretend they are the fresh home-made variety.

Rice

315 With improved production methods, there is no longer any need to wash rice. Washing often serves to clog the grains together right from the start, anyway, and certainly removes some of the nutrients. A little lemon juice or a slice of lemon added to rice during cooking keeps it white and grainy.

316 Easy-cook varieties of rice cost more and have less flavour. Use ordinary rice – long-grain or Basmati – and good results can be guaranteed if you first measure the rice and liquid by volume not weight, in a ratio of twice as much water or stock as rice. Put a teaspoon of oil, the lightly salted liquid and rice in the pan with the lid on and check that the heat is low. Let white rice cook for 15 minutes, brown for 40, and don't touch. (Stirring is the chief cause of glued rice because it damages the grains, and releases starch.) Put the pan aside for a couple of minutes once cooked, replacing the lid with a tea towel to draw the steam. Fluff the rice with a skewer rather than a fork.

A cup of uncooked grains will give 3 cups of cooked rice.

317 A teaspoon of oil added to the water when cooking rice makes it less likely to boil over.

318 The best and quickest way of making fried rice is to add *uncooked* grains of rice to a generous tablespoon of olive oil in a hot pan. Fry the grains for 1-2 minutes, stirring, then add liquid and cook by the boiling method *(see 316)*.

319 Keep rice hot by placing it in a pre-warmed and buttered bowl. Lay a folded cloth over this and cover with a lid which fits (if you have one, kitchen foil if you don't), and set the bowl over simmering water. It will keep hot for several hours like this if necessary.

320 Cooked rice will keep for 2-3 days if refrigerated, and can be reheated without even dirtying a pan. Pop it in a well-sealed 'roasting bag' (the kind sold for cooking meat joints and poultry without splattering the oven), and place this in boiling water to heat through.

321 Rice to be used cold in a salad should be cooled as quickly as possible after cooking. Spread it out in a thin layer on baking parchment or on a flat dish.

322 Salvage overcooked rice by adding a few sultanas, a small tin of evaporated milk and some sugar, and heating it through for rice pudding. On the other hand, you could pretend you meant it to be savoury rice, by adding a tin of drained, chopped Italian tomatoes, a dash of tomato purée, some chopped black olives and a few pine kernels. Top with breadcrumbs and pop under the grill.

323 Rice is often overlooked as a useful and tasty ingredient when making home-made soup. It can be added whole, and cooked as normal in the liquid; it can also be ground to a powder in a grinder, but in this case, add in the final stages of cooking.

Cereals

324 Some of the tastiest, crunchiest 'breadcrumbs' are made from leftover cereals – the corn or bran flake types – well crushed to crumb size.

325   The cheapest, most filling, and healthiest cereals are oat based. Make porridge for three good-sized helpings from one mug of oats, one mug of milk and one mug of water. Add a knob of butter or margarine to the pan first and a pinch of salt last to bring out the authentic Scots flavour. *(See also 498.)*

326   Make your own muesli. You may think it a drawback to buy a lot more than an average cereal packet in bulk, but cereals store well in screw-top jars or sealed packets. It's much more economical. You'll find a wide choice of ingredients at health stores.

> *5 mugs porridge oats*
> *5 mugs other grains mixed together (flaked barley, wheat-germ, jumbo oats etc.)*
> *1 mug chopped dates*
> *¹/₂ mug dried bananas or apricots*
> *¹/₂ cup sunflower seeds*
> *1 cup blanched peanuts*
> *¹/₂ cup hazelnuts*
> *¹/₄ cup sesame seeds*

Mix all the ingredients thoroughly in a large bowl. You can add optional extras or substitute for the above nuts and fruit. Try chopped pecan nuts, slivered almonds, chopped dried figs, pine kernels, cashews or walnuts.

327   Cereals which have become a little jaded can be crisped up again if placed for a few minutes on a baking tray in a warm oven. Otherwise crush them and use them as breadcrumbs *(see 324)* or add to meat loaves *(see 15 and 16)*.

Bread and Baking

Bread and Scones

328 Wipe a breadbin with a cloth sprinkled with vinegar, to prevent mildew. Place a washed and dried large potato in with the bread to keep it fresh.

329 When slicing bread, first dip the knife in boiling water and it will cut easily.

330 Bread which is a day or so old will taste freshly baked again if you run it quickly under the tap – top and bottom – and pop it in a hot oven for no more than a couple of minutes. Similarly, cut-price stale buns and scones can be salvaged if you brush them over with milk and place them in a hot oven for 2-3 minutes. Served with butter and jam, they'll taste freshly baked.

|331| Bread won't shrink so much in baking if you place a roasting tin half full of water on the floor of the oven. Brush the bread with salt water half-way through cooking for a crusty top.

|332| If there isn't a suitably warm corner in the kitchen where dough can rise, coat the inside of a plastic bag with a little oil, place the dough inside, seal the bag tightly and place in a bowl of warm water until the dough expands to twice the size.

|333| Cheat on a home-baked economy quick bread mix. Buy a 10oz (275g) packet of bread mix and add 4oz (100g) strong plain flour and a third more water than that specified in the packet instructions. You'll get up to six extra rolls.

|334| Never use a grill to make toast. You will recover the cost of a toaster before long in the amount of expensive energy saved. And you'll never have soggy toast again if you tap it all over with a spoon before placing it in the toast rack.

|335| Yesterday's fresh sliced loaf, now gone a little dry, makes perfect French toast. Allow 2 slices of bread, 1 egg, 4 table-spoons milk, 1 tablespoon sugar plus a knob of butter per person. Remove the crusts, mix the sugar and milk and beat the eggs. Dip the slices first in milk then in beaten egg and fry in hot butter until crisp and golden brown. Serve with a sprinkling of cinnamon, brown sugar or maple syrup. A delicious and nourishing breakfast or tea-time treat which children particularly love.

336 Turn stale bread into fresh breadcrumbs. Process for a few seconds in a mixer and pop into plastic bags or pots for the freezer. Toasted breadcrumbs are made from small chunks of bread, dried in the oven or under the grill. Place in a plastic bag and crush with a rolling pin. Frugal cooks make them with the remaining 'free' heat when the oven has been switched off after cooking.

337 Save time and distribute flavour evenly, when making ham or cheese sandwiches by mixing mustard into the softened butter before spreading. Meat, fish, cheese or egg sandwich fillings will go further if minced, grated or chopped first, and stirred into mayonnaise.

338 Pizzas make a popular and filling family dish, but are expensive when bought oven-ready and are often disappointing, with miserly, tasteless toppings. It's cheaper and more nutritious to buy packets of scone mix for a quick base. Add any topping – a smear of tomato paste or pesto on the base gives an authentic Italian flavour – such as chopped tinned tomatoes, lightly fried onion, grated Cheddar cheese or sliced Mozzarella, cooked chicken, chopped bacon, ham or frankfurters, tinned fish and olives, you name it . . . It's an ideal way to use up leftovers.

339 Flour your hands when working with dough to shape scones (and bread). You'll work faster as the dough won't stick to you. Add 3oz (75g) grated, full-flavoured Cheddar after the butter has been rubbed in for cheese scones, or make a herby batch by adding 2 tablespoons chopped parsley or 1 teaspoon dried herbs. Sprinkle the tops with sesame seeds, onion or celery salt before popping in the oven.

340 Scones will be lighter if soured milk rather than fresh is used *(see 269)*. Plain yoghurt as a substitute for milk is, some say, best of all.

Pastry

341 Cool-handed cooks get best results from pastry. Invest in a slab of marble to further ensure that the dough is kept at a low temperature during preparation.

342 To give pastry a lighter finish, and make it quicker to mix, grate hard fat from the fridge before adding to the flour. A little lemon juice added to the water when mixing pastry will make it extra light. Try soda water rather than plain water for short pastry. Dampen the baking sheet for a maximum rise in flaky or puff pastry. The steam created in the hot oven makes the layers of pastry rise faster and higher.

343 When making pastry to be served cold, use milk instead of water to moisten it. This way it will be shorter and stay crisper for longer.

344 Wine, vinegar or milk bottles make handy stand-ins for a rolling pin. In fact some cooks prefer them. You can fill a stoppered bottle with cold water when rolling pastry dough.

345 Keep a thin polythene bag beside you when making dough. Quickly slip your hand into it to answer the phone or open fridge and cupboard doors.

346 Newly made pastry should be allowed to rest in the fridge for 30 minutes before rolling and lining a flan tin. It should also rest after rolling to minimise shrinkage.

347 When making flan or pie pastry cases, roll out the dough to a circle 2 inches (5cm) larger than the tin in diameter. Butter the flan tins: this will help brown the pastry shell as well as making it easier to remove. After lining the flan tin or pie dish, quickly get rid of the overhanging edge by running a rolling pin over it.

348 If a pastry case cracks, seal it by brushing the seams with egg white and popping it back in the oven for a short while to set.

349 Brushed-on beaten egg glaze puts the finishing touches to golden pie crusts, but white vinegar is cheaper – brush it on 5 minutes before the end of cooking. You can cheat in an emergency where a cooked crust has simply refused to brown. Brush it over with a sugar and water solution, but keep an eye on it, it will now brown very quickly.

350 Pastry which is too crumbly for rolling can be converted to a crumble topping. Rub it over a grater and mix with cheese for a savoury topping, or with sugar and spices to cover fruit.

351 Made-up leftover pastry will keep for weeks in an airtight container in the fridge. Smaller pieces can be made into biscuits. Desiccated coconut or caster sugar can be kneaded into the pastry to give flavour and texture – it is then ready to roll into fingers or cut into shapes and bake on a baking sheet in the oven.

Biscuits

352 Choosing the right ingredients has a lot to do with successful biscuit baking. Best are caster sugar (rather than granulated), soft brown sugar (rather than demerara), and butter or block margarine, rather than the soft, easy-spread kind). Plain flour is the best to use, but you can replace a little of the recommended amount with cornflour where a shorter texture is called for.

353 Although part of the charm of home-baked biscuits lies in the fact that no two are alike, a more professional uniformity can be achieved at home. Instead of shaping by hand and transferring to trays, use the *back* of the baking sheet as a board. Flour it and roll the dough on it, then use a pastry cutter to cut the biscuits. Carefully remove the surplus dough from around each shape to leave undisturbed identical biscuits. Bake as usual.

354 Biscuits won't stick to the baking tray if you place the latter straight from the oven on to a wet cloth for a couple of minutes. (Do this to loosen small cakes too.)

355 Keep a few cubes of sugar in biscuit tins and they'll stay fresh and crisp.

356 Broken biscuits of the plain or digestive variety, crushed with a rolling pin, can be used for tasty biscuit-crumb bases for flans and cheesecakes. Per 8oz (225g) biscuit crumbs, add 4oz (100g) butter or marge and 1-2oz (25-50g) sugar. For quick and easy crushing, pop the biscuits in a plastic bag before rolling; or whizz in a blender.

Meringues

357 The best meringues are those made from eggs which have reached their sell-by date – i.e. *old* eggs – and they're usually knocked down in price too. Fresh eggs won't give such good results.

358 For guaranteed 'set-firm' meringues, add a teaspoon of corn-flour to the sugar before adding the egg whites. Or you could try a pinch of salt or a little cream of tartar.

359 To keep meringues soft, never exceed a ratio of 1oz (25g) sugar per white of egg. More sugar than that and they become hard, powdery and sickly. Add a pinch of baking powder (bicarbonate of soda) to egg whites before beating for extra rise. Add the sugar to meringues in two parts, whisking in up to half the total, then lightly folding the rest in with a metal spoon.

WHISK

360 It's imperative that the bowl you use to whisk egg whites for meringues is spotlessly clean without the slightest trace of grease. Rub it out with vinegar on kitchen paper, then do the same to the beater as an extra precaution before you start.

361 If you make meringues regularly, invest in a copper bowl. The coldness it produces increases the volume of white. Use a balloon whisk if a bowl is wide and shallow, a rotary whisk if it's deep and narrow.

362 To avoid meringues collapsing and looking exhausted as you produce them from the oven, lightly dust the tops with icing sugar before you put them in. Leave them a bit longer to rest with the heat switched off at the end of cooking time.

363 To cut a meringue cleanly, coat the knife with butter.

364 If, however hard you try, your meringues end up in pieces, arrange them decoratively with lashings of whipped cream and slivers of soft fruit for a scrumptious pudding. You needn't use them up straight away either: they'll keep for a couple of months wrapped in tin foil then stored in an airtight tin.

365 If meringues go a coffee-brown shade rather than the more desirable white or cream, try putting a wooden board under the baking tray next time.

Cakes

In General

366 Of course cakes won't stick if the tins are lined before baking. Prepare the tin before mixing the ingredients to avoid delaying the finished mixture reaching the oven. You can save a great deal of time and hassle by cutting through several layers of greaseproof paper in one go, so that you always have a stock of ready cut liners in the kitchen drawer. Tins greased with oil are less likely to stick than those greased with butter.

367 When filling the tin with a cake mix, make sure the mixture goes right into the corners by giving the tin a final sharp tap on a hard surface before placing it in the oven.

368 When flavouring cakes, don't use lemon juice if you want a light airy texture.

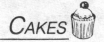
369 To avoid a cone-shaped cake, pour the batter all round the sides of the tin making a perceptible hollow in the middle. When the cake is put into the hot oven it will rise in the centre first, so by the time it is cooked, it will have a flat, even surface. (Cones of course can always be cut off to level the cake; you simply turn the cake over and ice the bottom instead.)

370 To test if a cake is properly cooked, insert a skewer in the middle. If it comes out cleanly, the cake is ready. If you haven't got a skewer, a strand of uncooked dried spaghetti will do.

371 To remove a cake easily from its tin after baking, place cake and tin in a basin of hot water. The heat will loosen it just sufficiently to be turned out. (Do not of course try this with a loose-bottomed cake tin!) Or stand the tin for a few moments on a damp tea towel and you'll be able to turn it out without damaging it.

372 When dividing a deep cake into layers, insert cocktail sticks at intervals around the middle to act as markers where you want the splits to be. It will then be easy to cut crossways, resting a serrated knife gently on the sticks to follow a straight line.

Fruit Cakes

373 Glacé cherries and other fruits used in baking won't sink to the bottom of the cake if they are first rinsed in hot water, spread on a kitchen towel to dry for a few minutes, then dusted with flour – take the flour out of the amount specified in the recipe. Add to the mix.

374 Soak currants in water or an alcohol before adding them to a cake and they will be plump, tender, and infinitely more succulent. Or place them in a sieve on top of a pan of boiling water to steam, shaking them occasionally. Spread them on absorbent paper to dry, or use a hair dryer.

375 Stop rich fruit cakes from burning at the bottom by placing the tin on layers of brown paper or newspaper on a baking sheet. Or place the tin inside a larger tin with two sticks across the bottom to raise it slightly. If the top browns before the inside is thoroughly cooked, cover the top with thick brown paper.

376 Make your own luxury cake flavouring using grated or finely chopped fresh orange or lemon peel. Place it in bottles and add a good quality brandy or runny honey and leave the skins to marinate in the liquid for several months. Ideal for fruit cakes, Christmas pudding, mince pies etc.

377 For orange and lemon peel flavourings in dried form, pound chopped peel up finely when it's been thoroughly dried in the oven, and store in a jar.

Sponge and Other Cakes

378 For quick and economical baking, buy a packet of best-quality cake mix and add to it 3 tablespoons self-raising flour, 1 generous tablespoon of caster sugar and the white of an egg. Mix with 3 dessertspoons more of water than recommended in the recipe, and now follow the instructions for baking. You should get up to a dozen extra small cakes.

379 To prevent a creamed cake mix curdling, and to give it a lighter texture, it's important to have fat and eggs at room temperature. As the oven has to be preheated anyway, sit the eggs on top of the stove until you are ready to use them. Sugar and fat will cream easily if the bowl is warmed first.

380 Whisk eggs and sugar over a bowl of hot water to ensure a well-risen sponge cake mix.

381 Don't despair over sunken sponge cakes. Treat them as one of life's trifles by breaking them up for a base, sprinkling them with orange juice or sherry, and topping with custard, cream, nuts and candied fruit. Or cut the middle out, and fill it with a mixture of fruit, pistachio nuts and whipped cream. Make 'angel' wings out of the sunken bit (simply cut in half), stick them back on top of the cream at an angle and lightly dredge the whole with icing sugar.

Cake Icing and Decorating

382 Mixing the sugar with milk rather than water makes icing thicker and therefore less inclined to run. Powdered milk will set it firmest of all. A teaspoon of glycerine added to each 1lb (450g) of icing sugar stops royal icing becoming too hard and crumbly.

383 Icing won't run down the sides if a cake is first lightly dredged with cornflour or arrowroot. Although they do the same job as plain flour they don't affect the taste.

384 To ensure that you can remove an iced cake from a tin sunny side up and unbroken, place the cake on the *lid* and fit the *bottom*, inverted, over it.

385 For a quick and inexpensive cake decoration, place a paper doily, one with a bold pattern rather than fiddly holes, on top of a sponge cake. Sift a layer of icing sugar over the whole thing. When the doily is carefully removed the icing sugar pattern remains.

386 Cover the top of a cake thickly with icing sugar and, using a hot skewer, brand lines on top. With a newly iced cake, a wire cooling rack becomes a useful decorating tool, producing an instant pattern when gently pressed on top. For a more elaborate design, fill in the squares with cherries, angelica, nuts or silver balls.

387 Fresh flowers – pansies, lily of the valley, violets, daisies etc. – and ribbons make quick and effective decorations for cakes. Dip the flower stalks under the heads in a little glycerine to help seal in moisture. Use a cocktail stick dipped in food colouring to add a hand-written message to the cake.

388 To decorate a cake with chocolate curls, use a potato peeler on a slab of well chilled chocolate. (In any case, chocolate keeps better longer when stored in the fridge.)

Puddings and Sweet Things

Hot and Cold Puds

389   Add a teaspoon of vinegar to the water in a saucepan when steaming puddings and the metal won't discolour.

390   Stop a skin forming on newly boiled custard by sprinkling sugar on top.

391   A teaspoon of cornflour added to egg yolks when preparing home-made custard prevents curdling.

392   Custard won't stick to the bottom of a pan which is first greased with buttered paper before the milk is poured in.

393 Dishes containing milk puddings should be placed in a tin of water in the oven to heat through gently without burning *(see 482)*.

394 For a quick-setting jelly, use only half the recommended amount of hot water to dissolve and add a sufficient number of ice cubes to make up the required amount of liquid.

395 A jelly will loosen easily and come out whole if the bowl or mould is dipped in hot water for just a couple of seconds.

396 Purée the good bits of damaged soft fruit with a small quantity of caster or icing sugar and use it as a saucy topping for ice cream, steamed sponge or rice pudding, or fold it into whipped cream for a fruit fool.

397 A batch of pancakes can be prepared in advance and kept separated by greaseproof paper. In a plastic bag in the fridge, they will stay fresh for up to 4 days, but they can also be frozen. For a quick dessert place a tablespoon of ice cream in the centre of each, fold in half and pour over a hot fruit sauce.

398 When preparing home-made ice cream deliberately over-do the flavouring and sweetening. Much of both will be lost in the freezing process. Don't serve home-made ice cream straight from the freezer or it will just be tasteless ice that's impossible to spoon. Allow it to soften in the fridge for up to an hour before serving. Never eat or refreeze melted ice cream.

399 Although this is not a recipe book, I felt I had to pass on this ambrosial pudding which has often saved my bacon over the years. Everybody likes it and a monkey or small child into elementary Lego could be employed as commis chef to help out when busy. Take a packet of biscuits: I prefer ginger snaps but the fruit and nut kinds are also good. Dip them in sherry and sandwich them together with whipped cream to form a log shape. Cover the top and sides with more cream and place in the fridge to chill and set firm for a few hours. Before serving, whip up more cream into which you have folded a stiffly whipped egg white, and coat the pudding with this light and frothy topping.

Decorate with chocolate curls *(see 388)*, maraschino cherries, and chocolate holly *(see 441)* if it's for a Christmas log. Good alternatives for decorating are slices of crystallised ginger, fresh strawberries, halved and de-seeded grapes, almonds or pistachio nuts.

Sweet Things

400 Don't waste money on caster or icing sugar. The grinder attachment on your blender will convert granulated sugar to caster in a couple of seconds, or to icing sugar if allowed to run for a little longer.

401 Keep a slice of apple in a canister of brown sugar and the sugar won't harden. A piece of bread in the container will also keep it fresh. Designer cooks put a few marshmallows with theirs.

402 Brown sugar which tends to go brick hard if exposed to the air for any length of time will separate and soften if left overnight in a bowl covered with a damp cloth. If you're in a hurry, break it up with a cheese grater.

403   Expert cake makers know the value of vanilla sugar. It gives a more subtle flavour than essence. All it needs is 2 whole vanilla pods: these will flavour a jar containing 2lb (900g) caster sugar when plunged into the centre. What's more, as you replace the sugar, the pods will go on flavouring it for months. Remove and use the pods themselves as needed, returning the rinsed and dried pods to the jar after use.

404   Honey which has crystallised and congealed in the jar will become smooth and runny again if placed in a pan of warm water and stirred until restored. The same applies to golden syrup.

405   If measuring honey or syrup by the spoonful, heat the spoon first, it will slide off more easily. Dust a bowl with flour or icing sugar before adding treacle, syrup or honey, and they won't stick so readily to the sides.

406   An easy way to measure a quantity of syrup, treacle or honey is to weigh the lidless tin or jar, subtract from that weight the amount needed for the recipe, and spoon out the syrup until you reach the lower figure.

407 Chocolate shouldn't be melted on a direct heat. To preserve texture and flavour, break chocolate up into small pieces in a heat-proof bowl and stand this in a pan of very hot water. Stir gently until melted. (Chocolate can be melted in the microwave without liquid.)

408 Add a tablespoon of oil, butter or marge to chocolate as it's melting, and it won't keep sticking to the spoon. It will also have a nice glossy appearance.

409 A chocolate sauce will have a piquant rather than sugary taste if red wine is used as a substitute for milk or water.

Jams and Preserves

Jams

410 Rub a little oil or butter round the inside of the preserving pan, and add a small pat of butter to the fruit when cooking, and it won't boil over.

411 Sugar should only be added in the later stages when the fruit is broken down and cooked through. Thereafter the jam should be boiled rapidly until set, but beware prolonged boiling once sugar is added. It darkens the colour and spoils the taste.

412 Jam has reached setting point if, when a small sample is spooned on to a cold plate and allowed to cool, it wrinkles when pushed with a finger.

413 If jam hasn't set, try returning it to the pan and adding extra lemon juice (or commercial pectin) and re-boiling. If nothing works, use the potential jam up as a fruit sauce *(see 396 and 397)*.

414 If jam is allowed to cool for a few minutes then given a brisk stir before being decanted into pots, any 'scum' which might have risen will be absorbed and the fruit won't rise to the top.

415 Stand jars on a wet cloth on top of a wooden chopping board and there will be no danger of them cracking as you slowly pour in the hot preserve. Warming them first, with hot water or in a cool oven, will also help.

416 Keep the wax paper from cereal wrappings for making jam jar seals. Using an upturned glass as a template, fold the paper over as many times as possible and cut a whole lot of circles in one go.

417 If wax paper is pressed well into the surface of the jam to exclude air, mould won't develop. A lemon-scented geranium leaf on top of the jam will also stop mould forming.

418 Good-quality cling film does a good job as a final seal for jam jars if lids are missing. White tissue paper brushed with egg white can seal the top of jam or marmalade; as the egg white hardens it protects against air and mould, so nothing else is needed.

Marmalades

419 If you haven't time to make marmalade when Seville oranges are at their cheapest and most plentiful in January and February, buy them anyway and freeze them whole until you can use them. Some pectin is lost in freezing, so whatever the amount stated in the recipe, add an eighth more of frozen oranges to compensate.

420 Although it may save time, mincing peel for marmalade, however coarsely, makes it mushy. Peel cut in even shreds gives the best results. This can be done the day before to spread the work load. An overnight soaking in water not only prevents the peel from drying out, but makes it softer.

421 Never discard the pips and membranes of oranges, as much of the essential pectin is stored there. Collect up in a muslin bag (or improvise with a large white handkerchief), and tie with string to the handle of the pan so that it can be easily removed, after the goodness has been cooked in with the fruit. Remove after the first cooking of 1-3 hours. Stir in the sugar and boil rapidly for a further 15-20 minutes until the marmalade reaches setting point. Although preserving sugar gives a clearer marmalade, many cooks prefer granulated for flavour. And for clarity, you can add a teaspoon of glycerine per 2lb (900g) of fruit, half-way through the cooking time.

Other Preserves

422 Smear a little salad oil on rubber rings for preserve jars. They'll stick better, but won't perish and can be used to re-seal another time. *Never* use metal tops on vinegar preserves; use plastic screw-on tops rather than film to prevent evaporation.

423 When making pickles or chutneys, never use utensils made of copper or brass, since vinegar reacts on them. Use only enamel, stainless steel or aluminium pans.

424 Make a wonderful chutney from your favourite apricot jam recipe by adding some vinegar, a little salt and cayenne pepper to taste. (Don't forget to 'cook' the stones with the jam, as the kernels add such flavour; tie them in a muslin bag, *see 421*.)

Entertaining

Special Occasions

425 Don't try out new dishes on guests. Choose a menu which you know is relatively easy and quick to prepare, balancing hot with cold and thinking about colours. It may sound obvious, but without proper planning, it's quite easy to serve a white soup followed by a white fish dish. A colourful tomato or spinach soup would be just as easy to prepare.

426 Make lists of everything, from the shopping you have to do, to a seating plan. Draw up a timetable. When you are rushed or nervous, this pre-planning takes away much of the worry and will help you avoid forgetting simple but essential tasks like pre-warming plates in the oven.

427   Try to plan a menu where as much as possible can be prepared in advance – a simple starter and a cold pudding perhaps or a main casserole dish which freezes well and just needs thawing and then heating through before serving. Fresh salads, stir-fry vegetables and hot bread are all quick and simple to prepare at the last minute.

428   Prepare the table and lay out oven-to-tableware first thing in the morning if possible. It's one chore less to do later, and you'll spot if any last-minute replacements are needed. Put cling film over small tables when necessary to avoid water marks from glasses, and kitchen foil under table cloths when children and the uncoordinated are invited.

429   Flowers and candles can be used to dramatic effect to produce a pretty table. Keep the candles in the fridge for about 24 hours before lighting to ensure they burn evenly and slowly, and don't drop wax. They will also keep the air fresh and clear of stale smoke. Make flower arrangements small. Beware of those the size of hedges where guests have to duck and dive round them to see each other, or which can't be moved without collapsing!

430   Make sure you won't run out of ice by preparing lots of ice cubes in advance. You don't need masses of ice trays. Buy a roll of disposable ice bags, or cheaper, use the bottom halves of plastic egg boxes half filled with water. Decant the ice into plastic bags for storage as each batch is ready.

431   For everyday eating where everyone's in a rush, instant coffee, ready-grated cheese in tubs and branded salad dressings are fine, but the effort taken to prepare from the best and freshest ingredients on a special occasion will be much appreciated. Freshly ground coffee and pepper, newly grated fresh Parmesan served with piping hot pasta, a hot home-prepared garlic or herb loaf, home-made mayonnaise or vinaigrette, all give the impression that you've taken the trouble and of course taste so very much better.

432 Busy cooks who enjoy entertaining, keep a note of what they served, to whom and when. They note that Daisy is a vegetarian, Samuel only eats kosher meat, Wanda is allergic to seafood and cheese gives Aunty Minnie migraine, etc. And where a meal is a particular success, they give it a star rating to cut down on hours of wondering and worrying in future.

Christmas

433 Don't let power cuts dampen the Christmas spirit – barbecue the turkey and eat it by candlelight.

434 If a frozen turkey is slow in defrosting, speed things up with the aid of a hair dryer.

435 The vexed question of how to lift a large bird out of a roasting tin has been solved by Tony de Angeli, editor of *The Grocer*. Take a 5 foot (1.5m) piece of string; fold it in half; tie the two ends together; tie two knots 10 inches (25 cm) from each end. Now put the string hammock into your roasting tin; place the turkey on top; and lift the loops so that the two ends of the bird go through them. Rest the string on top, and carry on cooking! When the moment comes, you will be able to lift out the turkey by holding the two loops. You may have to rock it a bit to dislodge it from the bottom.

436 Turkey, ham or other leftover cooked meat is eminently palatable when minced and mixed with melted butter, salt and pepper and any fresh herbs to taste. Serve with crusty bread and salad, or in sandwiches.

437 Dried fruit and candied peel still hanging around from last Christmas can be softened by soaking in boiling water and letting it sit for a few minutes.

438 Turn ordinary economy packs of mince pies into a de-luxe offering. Lift their lids and with a clean meat baster, squirt some brandy or rum into the centres before heating them through in the oven. Dust the tops with icing sugar and you can swear you made them yourself.

439 To take a pretty average Christmas cake into the luxury bracket, buy it, along with a miniature bottle of decent brandy, about a fortnight before Christmas. Use a thin skewer to poke holes in the cake and add the brandy in drips, getting it as deep into the holes as you can. A few days later, turn it over and repeat the procedure from the bottom. Repeat the process at intervals until the bottle is empty.

440 When a Christmas cake is mixed (just use your hands) and ready for the oven, cover it with a tea towel and leave it for 24 hours for maximum moisture and flavour.

441 Decorate Christmas cakes or puddings with chocolate holly leaves. Cover clean holly leaves with melted chocolate and put in the fridge to set. When solid, carefully peel off the leaf.

442 Add cold tea rather than beer to a Christmas pudding mix. Apart from the thrifty aspect, it stops the pud drying out and gives it a richer colour.

443 If, perchance, the Christmas pud emerges with all the softness and texture of a cannonball, slice it, fry it in butter and serve with sugar, cream and a big smile.

444 To keep your Christmas pudding flaming all the way to the table, heat both the serving plate and the brandy before you ignite the latter. Vodka is the stuff to add for a flavourless flambé. The alcohol content will set it alight but the liquor itself has no taste.

Drinks

Alcoholic and Non-Alcoholic

445 Unless properly chilled before opening, champagne will spray everywhere when the cork is released. If it does look like bubbling over, dip a wet finger in the top of the bottle. Any leftovers will keep until the next day if a teaspoon rather than a cork is placed in the top of the bottle with the handle hanging down inside.

446 Get into the habit of removing cheese from the fridge as you open red wine before a meal. The taste of both, even of the most inexpensive wine, will be greatly improved if allowed to breathe for a few hours.

447 Wine waiters finish pouring wine from a bottle with a rolling action and upward tilt of the bottle to save it dripping on people and table linen.

448 When making hot drinks to be poured into glasses – Gaelic coffee or mulled wine, for instance – the trick to prevent the glasses cracking is to first place a spoon in the glass. When filling several glasses together, it may be quicker and easier to just stand them on a damp cloth. To keep cream afloat in a Gaelic coffee, the hot liquid needs to be well sugared and the cream channelled slowly down a spoon until it slides on to the liquid inside the rim.

449 Half cans of fizzy drinks which have gone flat can be re-fizzed with a pinch of bicarbonate of soda and shaken before pouring.

450 Add the juice of a lemon to frozen orange juice in a blender and add the required amount of liquid to dilute. After whisking for just a few seconds it will be ready to serve and tastes like freshly squeezed juice.

451 Ice cube trays won't imbed themselves into the freezer compartment of a refrigerator if a sheet of kitchen foil or greaseproof paper is placed underneath them. Use a nutcracker to break up ice cubes small enough to fit into a vacuum flask for picnics.

452 A cork will fit any bottle if it is first boiled for 5 minutes to make it soft and pliable. Save the stoppers from sherry bottles – they make useful seals for wine bottles too.

453 A good substitute for a corkscrew is an ordinary screw with string attached round the head to pull out the cork.

454 To carry bottles home in the boot of the car without them clanking together and breaking, slip them inside old woolly socks!

Coffee, Tea and Chocolate

455 It may sound extravagant but the best coffee is made from still mineral water. Really boiling water spoils the flavour, so let boiled water cool slightly before adding to the grounds, granules or powder.

456 If percolated coffee has a strong overbrewed and bitter taste, add a pinch of salt.

457 It's simple to produce real coffee by pouring nearly boiling water on fresh grounds in an ordinary jug. Allow to brew for a couple of minutes, then add a tablespoon of cold water to the jug. The grounds will settle and stay undisturbed as you pour. If you only use freshly ground coffee as an occasional treat, it will keep for longer in the fridge, or you can buy a quantity of beans and freeze them.

458 Add a little grated chocolate to a cup of hot coffee and top with a tablespoon of whipped cream and a sprinkling of cinnamon for a velvety continental style drink. A half cup of coffee combined with a half cup of hot chocolate is also agreeably different.

459 Hot chocolate won't form a skin if you beat it in the pan to form a froth before pouring.

460   Herb teas are undoubtedly good for you, but you pay a lot for the pretty packaging. Make any amount of herbal teas from fresh herbs easily grown in gardens, tubs or window-boxes. Peppermint, rosemary, sage and camomile are among the most popular. Herbs can be dried on a baking tray in the bottom of a warm oven or between layers of kitchen paper in a microwave.

461   Although tins are the traditional containers, the flavour of tea improves greatly when it is stored in glass jars. Get rid of the musty smell in well-used tea pots with a salt and water solution, or add a teaspoon of bicarbonate of soda, fill to the rim with warm water, and leave overnight before rinsing well next morning.

In an Emergency

462 If you've forgotten to take an insulating bag with you to hold frozen food which may thaw on a long journey home, substitute newspapers.

463 In the event of a power cut, food will stay fresh for up to 8 hours in the freezer. If you have to unplug the freezer for any length of time – when moving house for instance – switch to 'fast freeze' for 24 hours before the move. Load it into the removal van last so that it can be plugged in, complete with the still frozen contents, as soon as you get to the new address.

464 If a chip pan catches fire, don't attempt to move it out of doors, and don't pour water on it. Turn off the heat and place a damp tea towel, tray or lid gently over the pan to exclude the air. Leave it to cool completely before uncovering. Prevention being the best policy, it's unwise to have a pan beyond a third full with fat, or more than half full with food added. Don't wait for a blue haze before adding food, and above all never leave the pan unattended.

465 If you can't think what to do with a roasting pan full of hot fat or dripping, save mess, blocked sinks and time by pouring it into an empty clean can. When it sets, it's easy to dispose of if it's old or rancid; or it can be kept in the fridge for another time.

466 If you've broken a glass or glass dish, sweep it up immediately. Don't risk cutting yourself on the tiny bits; use bread or damp cotton wool to pick them up safely.

467 If you've burned yourself slightly, run cold water over the affected part as soon as possible. Dry and dab with Vaseline – or egg white. (But always seek medical advice for more extensive burns.)

468 If you've burned the stew at the bottom, lift it from the heat and dip the pan bottom into cold water. This will persuade it to unstick itself. Scoop the unburned bits from the burned crust into another pan, and taste. If it's got a burned flavour, don't panic: cook a little chilli powder in some oil for a few minutes, then add the rescued remains and cook gently for a few more minutes before serving. The chilli powder will make the stew *hotter*, but it will mask the mistake!

Emergency Substitutes

469 If you haven't got any self-raising flour, just add 4 level tablespoons of baking powder per 2¼lb (1kg) plain flour. Mix well and pass through a sieve to ensure even blending.

470 When you suddenly realise you're out of gravy browning, add a dash of instant coffee.

471 Out of eggs and baking a cake? Replace the egg with a tablespoon of vinegar; the result will be the same, but the cost less, of course.

472 Tapioca is a useful standby for emergencies. When you're short of eggs, a tablespoon of tapioca soaked for a couple of hours in enough water to cover, will then bind rissoles and meat loaves, etc *(see 15 and 16)*.

473 A small piece of marrow bone makes a good stand-in for a misplaced pie funnel.

474 If you've lost the garlic crusher, chop the cloves roughly with a sharp knife, sprinkle salt on the fragments to draw the juices, and pound with the corner of a chopping board.

Essentials for Chief Cook and Bottle Washer

Gadgets and Equipment

475 If putting strong-smelling food in a vacuum flask that has a cork stopper, cover the stopper with cling-film first, to prevent it absorbing the smell.

476 Place a sheet of emery paper on a board, wrapping it over the edges of the wood, and tack it down. Sharpen the blades of kitchen knives on it. Cutting through emery paper a few times will sharpen kitchen scissors, as will using them as if trying to cut the neck off a milk bottle. About 20 times will give a good cutting edge.

477 A round chopping board covered in kitchen foil doubles as a good solid cake stand.

478 When shopping for saucepans, it's a good idea to buy enamel dishes and saucepans with lids which are same size. One can then slot on top of the other, warming the food on top of that which is boiling below, thus saving space *and* fuel.

479 A proper steamer – a perforated lidded pan over another pan – is expensive to buy, but so useful, and steamed food is healthy. Improvise with a colander and close-fitting lid over a suitably sized saucepan.

480 Asparagus pans are an extravagance. Tie the bundle of trimmed asparagus together, wrap the tips gently in foil, and cook in an enamel or other heatproof coffee pot. This has the height needed for the spears!

481 Metal baking sheets are useful for a variety of things. If you place a small one over a cooker ring, this will distribute the heat and you can cook food in two small saucepans at the same time. Putting flan dishes on a preheated metal tray in the oven speeds up the conduction of heat through the pastry of a pie or quiche. Soufflés will rise quicker if the dish is placed on a hot tray.

482 A bain-marie is useful for many dishes which need ultra gentle cooking, whether in the oven or on top of the stove (milk puddings, for example). Improvise with a baking or roasting tin and fill with warm water to come half-way up the sides of the dish or dishes holding the food. For even more protection, place newspaper in the water in the bain-marie and the dish on top.

483 New non-stick frying pans should carry manufacturers' instructions for treating them before use. Otherwise heat a layer of salt in the bottom and rub round with kitchen paper to clean and condition the surface. After each use, wipe clean with a spot of cooking oil on kitchen paper. Protect with a layer of cling film or hang up to store.

|484| Bright and shiny baking tins made from tin are fairly inexpensive, and quite effective. Choose well-made tins with few seams which could harbour food remnants. To prevent them rusting, rub with fresh lard and thoroughly heat in the oven before using. After washing, rub them over with a cloth dampened with an ammonia and water solution, and dry thoroughly.

|485| A freezer pays enormous dividends through allowing you to take advantage of bulk buys, seasonal offers and batch cooking, which saves time and money. Defrost twice a year – this can save up to 10% of its running costs *(see 490)*.

|486| A liquidiser is an excellent investment, not least where there are small children. Save fortunes on baby foods, make cheap and nourishing drinks with bananas and honey, or blend together half a cup each of yoghurt and milk. Whisk up delicious soups from less than perfect vegetables and home-made stock.

|487| Oven-to-table ware is very useful, and has become understandably popular in modern times, but even the effect can be ruined by cooking spills. Wipe them off with salt on the dampened edge of a tea towel before serving.

|488| Keep cut-out recipes clean whilst cooking by using a photo album. There are usually plenty to choose from in the sales, and the plastic covers are perfect see-through protection.

Cleaning and Washing Up

|489| Fridges and freezers, if left unused and closed, will attract mould. When in use, leave a lump of charcoal in both to draw moisture and act as a deodoriser.

490 To clean a freezer, use mild detergent suds and a dash of household bleach. Rinse thoroughly with clear water well laced with vinegar to dispel all traces of mould or mildew. When thoroughly dry, rub round the inside surface with glycerine on a soft cloth to make it quick and easy to defrost again when necessary. To run efficiently and economically, a freezer must be defrosted regularly, say every six months. It should always be kept full too, fill the gaps with ice blocks or cubes, or even crumpled newspaper.

491 Although baking powder (bicarbonate of soda) is one of the most useful ingredients, it will eventually run out of fizz if stored for too long. If in doubt about its efficacy, test a teaspoon in ½ pint (300ml) hot water. If it's still effervescent, use it in cooking; if flat as a pancake, use it for cleaning the silver, the bathroom taps, the dog's teeth or any of the dozens of other jobs it performs as a household cleanser and de-odoriser. No kitchen can be without it. *(See 492 and 501.)*

492 Bicarbonate of soda used as a 'sealer' on a newly cleaned oven makes next time round child's play. Use a strong solution – at least 1 tablespoon to ½ pint (300ml) water – and apply a light film over all the surfaces. This can be used as a cleaner as well. Leave for an hour, then wipe off. It's particularly good on glass oven doors.

493 Caustic soda is cheaper than proprietary brands of oven cleaner and generally more severe, so it works well on really revolting ovens. Follow the manufacturer's instructions care-fully. Add the caustic soda to the water and not the other way round or the mixture will fizz up alarmingly. Wear rubber gloves and wash any accidental splashes off immediately with generous amounts of cold water. Ventilate the room well and avoid inhaling the fumes.

494 Marble slabs, beloved of pastry cooks, are useful too as a cool platter on which to arrange food in hot weather. They can be easily cleaned and the colour restored with a bucket of water containing 2 tablespoons of vinegar. Any stains will shift after a good rub with salt applied on the surface of a cut lemon; leave to soak for half an hour before rinsing.

495 Quickest way to clean dirt-encrusted knobbly bits and rings on cookers is to pop them into a stout dustbin liner and carry the bag outdoors. Pour in a couple of cups of household ammonia and seal the top of the bag. When the solution, with its pungent fumes contained, has done the work for you, the loosened grime can be simply washed off with a garden hose.

496 Chopping boards are a major breeding ground for harmful bacteria and must always be given a final rinse with very hot water. When newly cleaned, rub salt or a cut lemon into the wood to deodorise and bleach.

497 Clean a food mixer quickly by squirting some washing-up liquid into one-third the vessel's capacity of water and switching on for a few seconds. Repeat with cold water to rinse. Where a liquidiser or food mixer has been used for strong smelling food such as fish, add a drop of lemon or vinegar to the rinse to deodorise. It will also remove any traces of oil.

498 Porridge pots are amongst the most difficult to clean. Fill the pot immediately with cold water and then stand it on the still warm but not heated stove. The porridge will loosen from the bottom and sides and then can be easily scraped out. The same method applies to other notoriously adhesive foods, scrambled eggs for example. Another alternative is to soak the pan overnight with lukewarm water in which you've dissolved a tablespoon of biological washing powder.

499 Aluminium pans can be easily cleaned by adding an onion to water in the pan and bringing it to the boil. The burnt matter will rise to the top leaving the saucepan bright and clean again. Or boil a tablespoon of salt and an equal amount of barley in the soiled pan.

500 Banish strong fish smells from pans and cooking utensils by emptying tea leaves from the pot into the pan, half filling with lukewarm water and leaving to soak while you finish the rest of the washing-up. Use cold rather than hot water to wash and rinse. You could also add lemon juice, vinegar or coffee grounds to water in the pan. Bring to the boil before pouring away and rinsing well.

501 Remove fish odour from hands by rubbing them with dry mustard powder or bicarbonate of soda. Mustard is also the secret of deodorising fishy silverware: add a teaspoon of mustard powder to the washing-up water. Rub other utensils with lemon rind.